SPPU New Syllabus

AF897910

A Book Of

WEB TECHNOLOGY

(HTML-JSS-CSS)

For B.B.A.(Computer Application) : Semester - II

[Course Code 205 : Credit - 3]

CBCS Pattern

As Per New Syllabus, Effective from June 2019

Mr. Bhupesh Taunk
MSc(Computer Science)
Lecturer, Computer Science Department
Fergusson College, Pune

Mr. Aniket Nagane
M.Sc.(Computer Science),NET
Asst. Professor Computer Science Department
MIT Group of Institutions
MAEER's Arts, Commerce and Science College
Alandi(D), Pune

NIRALI PRAKASHAN
ADVANCEMENT OF KNOWLEDGE

N4945

Web Technology (HTML-JSS-CSS) **ISBN 978-93-89686-96-8**

First Edition : January 2020

Published By :

NIRALI PRAKASHAN

Abhyudaya Pragati, 1312, Shivaji Nagar,
Off J.M. Road, Pune – 411005
Tel - (020) 25512336/37/39, Fax - (020) 25511379
Email : niralipune@pragationline.com

➢ DISTRIBUTION CENTRES

PUNE

Nirali Prakashan (For orders within Pune) : 119, Budhwar Peth, Jogeshwari Mandir Lane, Pune 411002, Maharashtra
Tel : (020) 2445 2044; Mobile : 9657703145
Email : niralilocal@pragationline.com

Nirali Prakashan (For orders outside Pune) : S. No. 28/27, Dhayari, Near Asian College Pune 411041
Tel : (020) 24690204; Mobile : 9657703143
Email : bookorder@pragationline.com

MUMBAI

Nirali Prakashan : 385, S.V.P. Road, Rasdhara Co-op. Hsg. Society Ltd.,
Girgaum, Mumbai 400004, Maharashtra; Mobile : 9320129587
Tel : (022) 2385 6339 / 2386 9976, Fax : (022) 2386 9976
Email : niralimumbai@pragationline.com

➢ DISTRIBUTION BRANCHES

JALGAON

Nirali Prakashan : 34, V. V. Golani Market, Navi Peth, Jalgaon 425001, Maharashtra,
Tel : (0257) 222 0395, Mob : 94234 91860; Email : niralijalgaon@pragationline.com

KOLHAPUR

Nirali Prakashan : New Mahadvar Road, Kedar Plaza, 1st Floor Opp. IDBI Bank, Kolhapur 416 012
Maharashtra. Mob : 9850046155; Email : niralikolhapur@pragationline.com

NAGPUR

Nirali Prakashan : Above Maratha Mandir, Shop No. 3, First Floor,
Rani Jhanshi Square, Sitabuldi, Nagpur 440012, Maharashtra
Tel : (0712) 254 7129; Email : niralinagpur@pragationline.com

DELHI

Nirali Prakashan : 4593/15, Basement, Agarwal Lane, Ansari Road, Daryaganj
Near Times of India Building, New Delhi 110002 Mob : 08505972553
Email : niralidelhi@pragationline.com

BENGALURU

Nirali Prakashan : Maitri Ground Floor, Jaya Apartments, No. 99, 6th Cross, 6th Main,
Malleswaram, Bengaluru 560003, Karnataka; Mob : 9449043034
Email: niralibangalore@pragationline.com

Other Branches : Hyderabad, Chennai

Preface ...

We take this opportunity to present this book entitled as **"Web Technology (HTML-JSS-CSS)"** to the students of Second Semester - BBA (Computer Application). The object of this book is to present the subject matter in a most concise and simple manner. The book is written strictly according to the New Syllabus (CBCS Pattern).

The book has its own unique features. It brings out the subject in a very simple and lucid manner for easy and comprehensive understanding of the basic concepts, its intricacies, procedures and practices. This book will help the readers to have a broader view on Web Technology (HTML-JSS-CSS). The language used in this book is easy and will help students to improve their vocabulary of Technical terms and understand the matter in a better and happier way.

We sincerely thank Shri. Dineshbhai Furia and Shri. Jignesh Furia of Nirali Prakashan, for the confidence reposed in us and giving us this opportunity to reach out to the students as well as teachers.

We have given our best inputs for this book. Any suggestions towards the improvement of this book and sincere comments are most welcome on niralipune@pragationline.com.

Authors

■■■

Syllabus ...

1. Introduction **[05 Lectures]**

1.1 Clients- Servers and Communication
1.2 Internet-Basic, Internet Protocols (HTTP, FTP, IP)
1.3 World Wide Web (WWW)
1.4 HTTP request message, HTTP response message

2. Web Design **[09 Lectures]**

2.1 Concepts of effective Web Design
2.2 Web Design issues including Browser Bandwidth and Cache
2.3 Display Resolution
2.4 Look and Feel of the Website
2.5 Page Layout and linking
2.6 User Centric Design
2.7 Sitemap
2.8 Planning and Publishing Website
2.9 Designing Effective Navigation

3. HTML **[12 Lectures]**

3.1 Introduction to HTML
3.2 Basic HTML Structure
3.3 Common HTML Tags
3.4 Physical and Logical HTML
3.5 Types of Images, Client Side and Server-Side Image Mapping
3.6 List, Table, Frames
3.7 Embedding Audio, Video
3.8 HTML Form and Form Elements
3.9 Introduction to HTML Front Page

4. Style Sheets **[10 Lectures]**

4.1 Need for CSS
4.2 Introduction to CSS
4.3 Basic Syntax and Structure
4.4 Using CSS:
  4.4.1 Background Images, Colors and Properties,
  4.4.2 Manipulating Texts, Using Fonts, Borders and Boxes, Margins, Padding Lists, Positioning using CSS
4.5 Overview and Features of CSS2 and CSS3

5. JavaScript **[12 Lectures]**

5.1 Introduction to JavaScript
5.2 Identifier & Operator, Control Structure, Functions
5.3 Document Object Model (DOM),
5.4 DOM Objects (Window, Navigator, History, Location)
5.5 Predefined Functions, Math & String Functions
5.6 Array in JavaScripts
5.7 Event handling in JavaScript

■■■

Contents ...

1...

Introduction

Objectives...

- To learn Client – Server Model.
- To study Internet basic and Internet Protocols (HTTP, FTP, IP).
- To understand World Wide Web (WWW).
- To study HTTP Request Message and HTTP Response Message.

1.1 INTRODUCTION

- Nowadays, Web Technologies have become an essential part of everyday of our daily life. Web technologies are used in Education, Government, Banking, Social Networking (Facebook, Twitter, etc.) and so on.
- Web Technology is the establishment and use of mechanisms that make it possible for different computers to communicate and share resources.
- Web Technology provides a platform for effective communication among different users and devices on a computer network.
- Web Technologies are related to the interface between web servers and their clients. This information includes markup languages, programming interfaces, languages and standards for document identification and display.
- In this chapter, we discuss web essential concepts.

1.1.1 Basic Terms Related to Web Technologies

- Some important terms related to Web Technologies are discussed below:
  1. **WWW:** The World Wide Web abbreviated as WWW or W3 and commonly known as the Web. WWW is a system of interlinked hypertext documents accessed via the Internet. With a web browser, one can view web pages that may contain text, images, videos, and other multimedia, and navigate between them via hyperlinks.
  2. **HyperText Markup Language (HTML):** It is the main markup language for displaying web pages and other information that can be displayed in a web browser
  3. **Website:** Website is a set of related web pages containing content such as text, images, video, audio, etc. A website is hosted on at least one web server, accessible via a network such as the Internet or a private local area network through an

Internet address known as a Uniform Resource Locator (URL). All publicly accessible websites collectively constitute the World Wide Web (WWW).

4. **Web Application:** A web application or web app is any software that runs in a web browser. It is created in a browser-supported programming language such as the combination of JavaScript, HTML, CSS etc. and relies on a web browser to render the application.

5. **Web Pages:**
   - A web page is a document, typically written in plain text distributed with formatting instructions of HyperText Markup Languages like HTML, XHTML.
   - A webpage may incorporate elements from other websites with suitable markup anchors.
   - The pages of a website can usually be accessed from a simple Uniform Resource Locator (URL) called the web address.
   - HTML documents describe web pages. HTML documents contain HTML tags and plain text. HTML documents are also called web pages.
   - There are two types of web pages i.e., static and dynamic.

   (i) Static Web Pages:
   - A static web page sometimes called a flat page/stationary page.
   - A static web page is a web page that is delivered to the user exactly as stored.
   - Static web page displays the same information for all users, from all contexts, subject to modern capabilities of a web server to negotiate content-type or language of the document where such versions are available and the server is configured to do so.
   - Static web pages are often HTML documents stored as files in the file system and made available by the web server over HTTP.

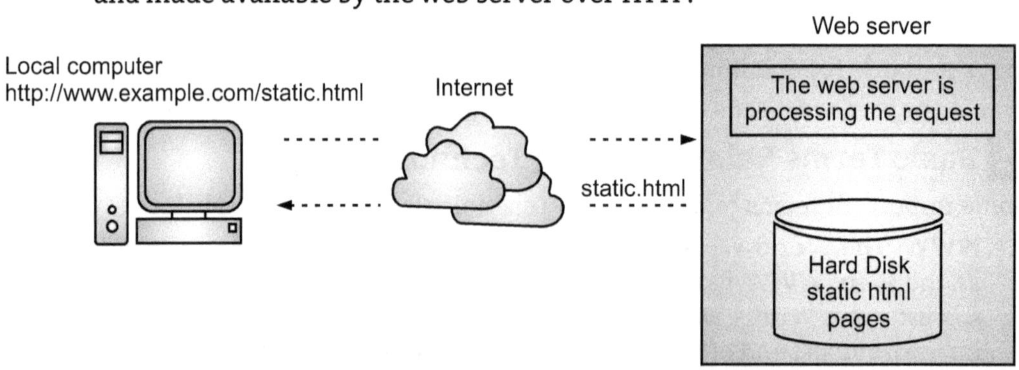

Fig. 1.1: Static Web Page is delivered to the user exactly as stored

Advantages:
- Quick and easy to put together, even by someone who does not have much experience.
- Ideal for demonstrating how a site will look.
- Cache friendly, one copy can be shown to many people.

Disadvantages:

- Difficult to maintain when a site gets large.
- Difficult to keep consistent and up to date.
- Offers little visitor personalization (all would have to be client side).

(ii) Dynamic Web Pages:

- A dynamic web page is a web page with web content that varies based on parameters provided by a user or a computer program.

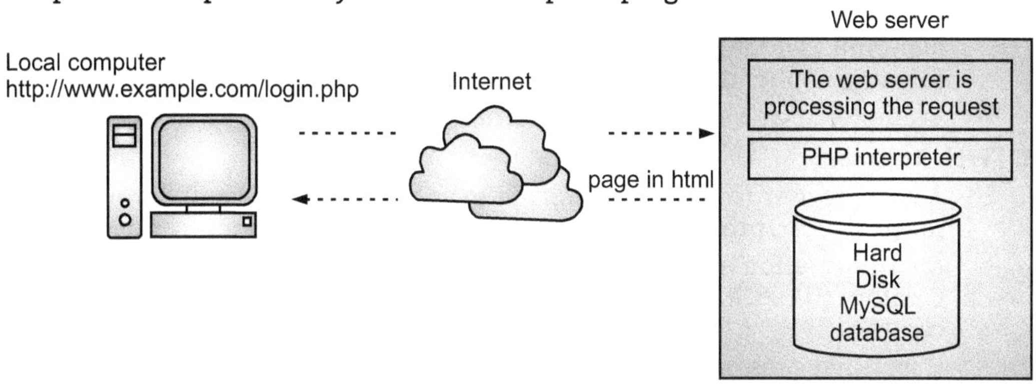

Fig. 1.2: Example of dynamic web page Server-Side scripting (PHP and MySQL)

- Typically written in various scripting languages or technologies such as ASP, PHP, Perl or JSP.

Advantages:

- Offers highly personalized and customized visitor options.
- Database access improves the personalized experience.
- Scripts can read in data sources and display it differently depending on how it is run.

Disadvantages:

- Personalized pages are not very cache friendly.
- Requires a basic minimum knowledge of the language being used.
- Scripts need more consideration when uploading and installing, particularly to Unix-related servers.

6. **Web Publishing:**
   - Web publishing, or "online publishing," is the process of publishing content on the Internet.
   - It includes creating and uploading websites, updating webpages, and posting blogs online and the published content may include text, images, videos, other types of media.
   - In order to publish content on the web, we need three things:
     (i) Web development software.
     (ii) An Internet connection.
     (iii) A web server.

- The software may be a professional web design program like Dreamweaver or a simple web-based interface like WordPress.
- The Internet connection serves as the medium for uploading the content to the web server.
- Large sites may use a dedicated web host, but many smaller sites often reside on shared servers, which host multiple websites.

7. **Web Server:**
    - The web is a collection of files known as web pages. Web pages can contain hyperlinks which point to other web pages. The web pages can be viewed with software application known as a web browser.
    - Examples of web browsers are Internet Explorer, Netscape and Opera etc.

8. **Web Browser:**
    - A web browser (commonly referred to as a browser) is a software application for retrieving, presenting and traversing information resources on the WWW.
    - An information resource is identified by a Uniform Resource Identifier/ Locator (URI/URL) and may be a web page, image, video or other piece of content.
    - Hyperlinks present in resources enable users easily to navigate their browsers to related resources.

1.2 CLIENTS-SERVERS AND COMMUNICATION [S-19, 16]

1.2.1 Client-Server Model

- Client-Server Model is a technology which is based on distribution of task or function between two independent processes i.e. client and server.
- Client-Server model is a concept for describing communications between computing processes that are classified as service consumers (clients) and service providers (servers).
- Following are the two parts of the client-server models:
- **Client:** It is a process or a computer in network that request services from a server process.
- **Server:** It is a process or a computer in network that serves or provides the requested services (response) to client process.

Types of Clients and Servers:

- Depending on the amount of processing carried out type of Client and Server can be decided.
    1. **Thin Client:** When minimum processing is done at client side it is called as Thin Client.
    2. **Fat Server:** When maximum processing needs to be carried out at server due to thin client, such servers are called as Fat Servers.
    3. **Fat Client:** When maximum processing is done at client side it is called as Fat Client.
    4. **Thin Server:** When minimum processing needs to be carried out at server due to thin clients such servers are called as Thin Servers.

- **Specific types of clients include:** Web browsers, E-mail clients, and online chat clients.
- **Specific types of servers include:** Web Servers, FTP servers, database servers, E-mail servers,
- Fig. 1.3 represents a simple Client-Server Model.
- The client–server model partitions tasks placed between the providers of a resource or service, called servers, and service requesters, called clients.

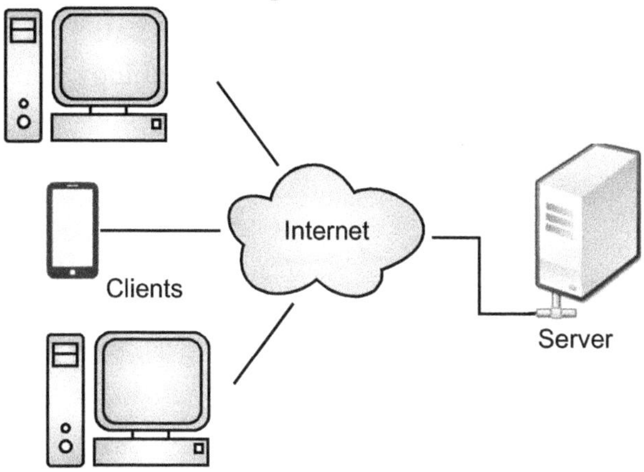

Fig. 1.3: A simple Client-Sever Model

- **Example:** When a bank customer accesses online banking services with a web browser (the client), the client initiates a request to the bank's web server. The customer's login credentials may be stored in a database, and the web server accesses the database server as a client. An application server interprets the returned data by applying the bank's business logic, and provides the output to the web server. Finally, the web server returns the result to the client web browser for display.
- In each step of this sequence of client-server message exchanges, a computer processes a request and returns data. This is the request-response messaging pattern. When all the requests are met, the sequence is complete and the web browser presents the data to the customer.

Advantages of Client-Server Model:

1. Centralized servers are more stable.
2. Security is provided through the server.
3. New technology and hardware can be easily integrated into the system.
4. Servers are able to be accessed remotely from different locations and types of systems.

Disadvantages of Client-Server Model:

1. Cost of buying and running a server are high.
2. Dependence on a central location for operation.
3. Requires regular maintenance and updates.

1.2.2 Communication in Client-Server

- The communication in clients and servers exchange messages in a request-response messaging pattern.
- The client sends a request, and the server returns a response. This exchange of messages is an example of inter-process communication.
- To communicate, the computers must have a common language, and they must follow rules so that both the client and the server know what to expect. The language and rules of communication are defined in a communication protocol.
- Fig. 1.4 shows a simplified view of client-server technology. Client requests information from the server and server responds with the information.

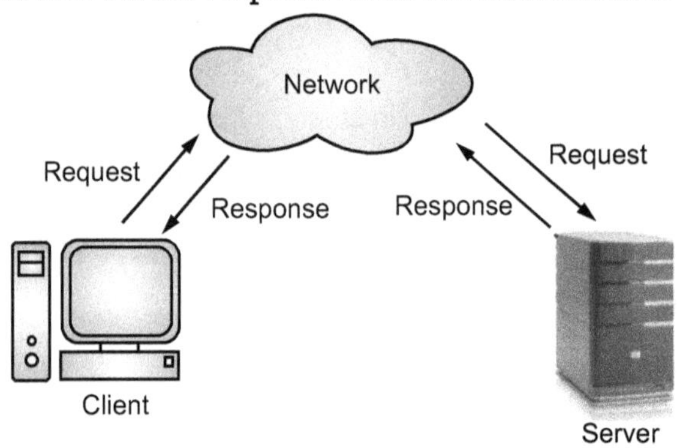

Fig. 1.4: Simplified view of Client-Server Technology

1.3 INTERNET BASICS [W-17, 16, S-19, 17]

- The Internet is a global system of interconnected computer networks that use the standard Internet Protocol suite (TCP/IP) to link several billion devices world wide.
- The TCP/IP Internet Protocols, a common example, consist of, Transmission Control Protocol (TCP), which uses a set of rules to exchange messages with other Internet points at the information packet level. Internet Protocol (IP), which uses a set of rules to send and receive messages at the Internet address level.
- Internet is a network that consists of millions of private, public, academic, business, and government networks of local to global scope, linked by a broad array of electronic, wireless, and optical networking technologies.
- Internet (Net or Web) is a massive distributed client-server information system as represented in the Fig. 1.5.

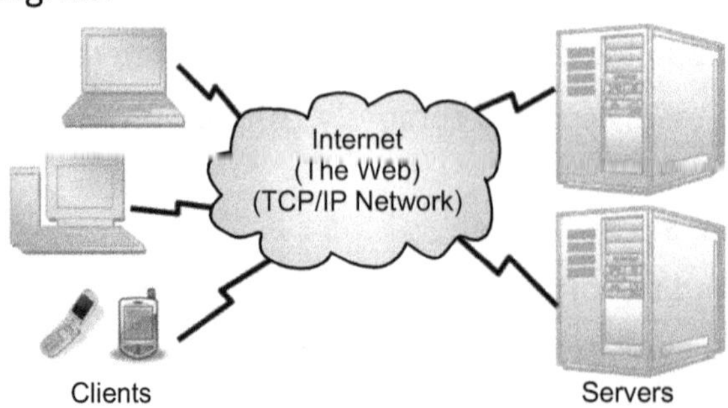

Fig. 1.5: Client-Server Information System

- Many applications are running concurrently over the web, such as web browsing/ surfing, E-mail, file transfer, audio and video streaming, and so on. In order for proper communication to take place between the client and the server, these applications must agree on a specific application-level protocol such as HTTP, FTP, SMTP, POP etc.

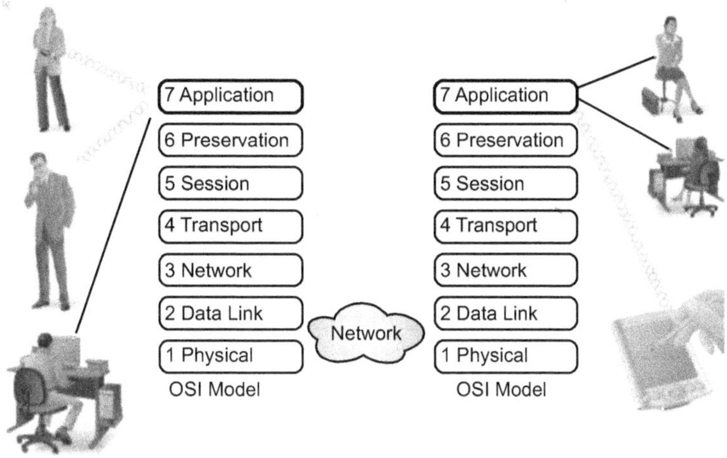

Fig. 1.6: Interface between Application Layer and Network

- Fig. 1.7 describes some of the Internet's capabilities.

Image	Function	Description
	Communication and Collaborate	Send electronic mail messages; transmit documents and data; participate in electronic conferences.
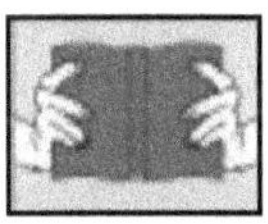	Access Information	Search for documents, databases, and library card catalogs; read electronic brochures, manuals, books and advertisements.
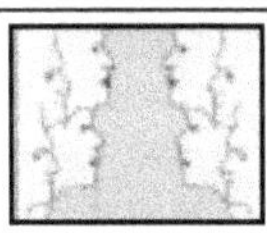	Participate in Discussions	Join interactive discussion groups; conduct voice transmission.
	Supply Information	Transfer computer files of text, computer programs, graphics, animations, sound or videos.
	Find Entertainment	Play interactive video games; view short video clips; listen to sound and music clips; read illustrated and even animated magazines and books.
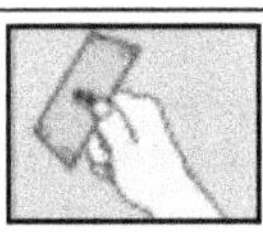	Exchange Business Transactions	Advertise, sell and purchase goods and services.

Fig. 1.7: Internet's Capabilities

1.4 INTERNET PROTOCOLS [S-18]

- The Web is one of several ways to retrieve information from the Internet. These different types of Internet connections are known as protocols.
- A protocol is a set of rules that governs data communications. It represents an agreement between the communicating devices. Without a protocol, two devices may be connected but not communicating.
- The Internet protocols are the world's most popular open-system (non-proprietary) protocol suite because they can be used to communicate across any set of interconnected networks.
- Internet protocols include TCP (Transfer Control Protocol), IP (Internet Protocol), HTTP (HyperText Transfer Protocol), FTP (File Transfer Protocol), and so on.

1.4.1 HTTP (HyperText Transfer Protocol) [W-17, S-17]

- The HTTP is a protocol that is used to define how the client-server programs can be written to retrieve web pages from the Web.
- An HTTP client sends a request and HTTP server returns a response.
- HTTP is a connection-oriented and reliable protocol.
- HTTP is the foundation of the modern web. HTTP is at the heart of the Web. It is described in [RFC 1945] and [RFC 2616].
- HTTP is a stateless protocol. In other words, the current request does not know what has been done in the previous requests.
- HTTP permits negotiating of data type and representation, so as to allow systems to be built independently of the data being transferred.
- HTTP defines that how web browser communicate with web server. On Web, for a browser request the HyperText Transfer Protocol (HTTP) is used.
- HTTP defines methods for the client-server communication as shown in Fig. 1.8.

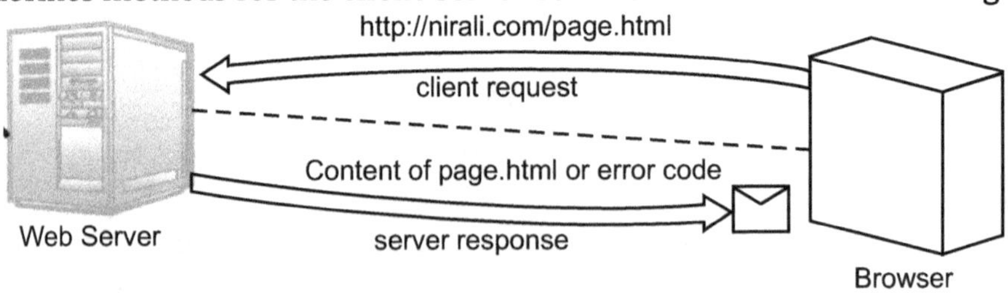

Fig. 1.8: Methods for Client-Server Communication

1.4.2 FTP (File Transfer Protocol) [W-16, S-18, 16]

- Data exchange has been important from the early days of computing. A popular means of data exchange is connecting computers to one another.
- The FTP is used to transfer files between two computers over a Network and Internet. FTP is described in RFC 959.
- FTP can transfer files between any computers that have an Internet connection, and also works between computers using totally different operating systems. FTP uses the Internet's TCP/IP protocols to enable data transfer.

- FTP protocol falls within a client-server model, i.e. one machine sends orders (the client) and the other awaits requests to carry out actions (the server).
- Transferring files from a client computer to a server computer is called "uploading" and transferring from a server to a client is "downloading".

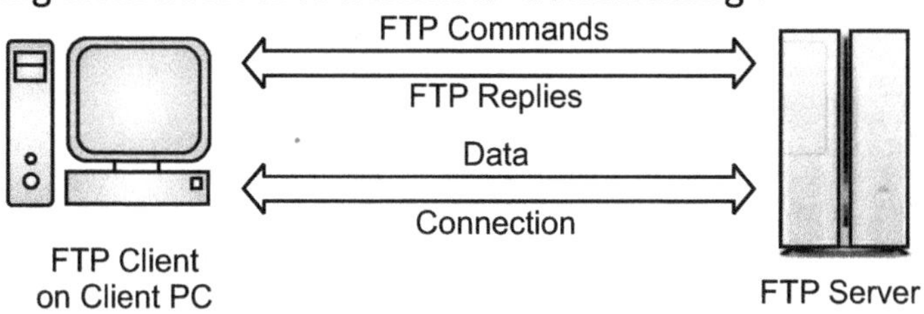

Fig. 1.9: File Transfer Protocol

1.4.3 IP (Internet Protocol)

- IP is the primary network protocol used on the Internet, developed in the 1970s.
- IP is the fundamental building block for all control and data exchanges across and within the Internet.
- Internet is the collection of all networked computers that interoperate using IP, IP as the protocol that facilities communication between computers within the Internet.
- IP is an unreliable, connectionless protocol. IP is documented in RFC 791.
- The Internet Protocol (IP) is the method or protocol by which data is sent from one computer to another on the Internet. Each computer (known as a host) on the Internet has at least one IP address (unique identifier) that uniquely identifies it from all other computers on the Internet.
- The Internet Protocol is responsible for addressing hosts and for routing datagrams (packets) from a source host to a destination host across one or more IP networks. For this purpose, the IP defines the format of packets and provides an addressing system that has two functions: identifying hosts; and providing a logical location service
- The first major version of IP, Internet Protocol Version 4 (IPv4), is the dominant protocol of the Internet. Its successor is Internet Protocol Version 6 (IPv6).
- Fig. 1.10 shows IP provides a uniform network layer protocol to operate over any collection of data link protocols and physical links.

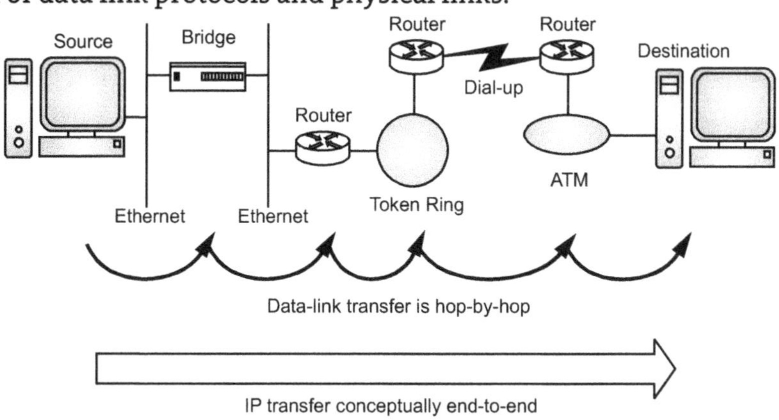

Fig. 1.10: Internet Protocol

1.5 WORLD WIDE WEB (WWW) [W-16]

- The term WWW refers to the World Wide Web or simply the Web.
- The World Wide Web consists of all the public websites connected to the Internet world wide, including the client devices (such as computers and cell phones) that access Web content.
- The WWW is just one of many applications of the Internet and computer networks.
- WWW is defined as "the type of system designed for the hyper text documents that are used with the help of internet technology for the purpose of searching and for different purposes of the benefit of the mankind".

Working of WWW:

- World Wide Web works on the client-server model.
- A user computer works as a client which can receive and send data to the server.
- When a web page is requested by a user, the browser contacts the requested server (where the website is stored) and by fetching and interpreting the requested files, it displays the web page on the computer screen.
- Information is stored in documents called web pages and the web pages are files stored on computers called web servers.
- Computer reading the web pages are called web clients. Web clients view the pages with a program called a web browser.
- Fig. 1.11 shows working of WWW Client-Server model.

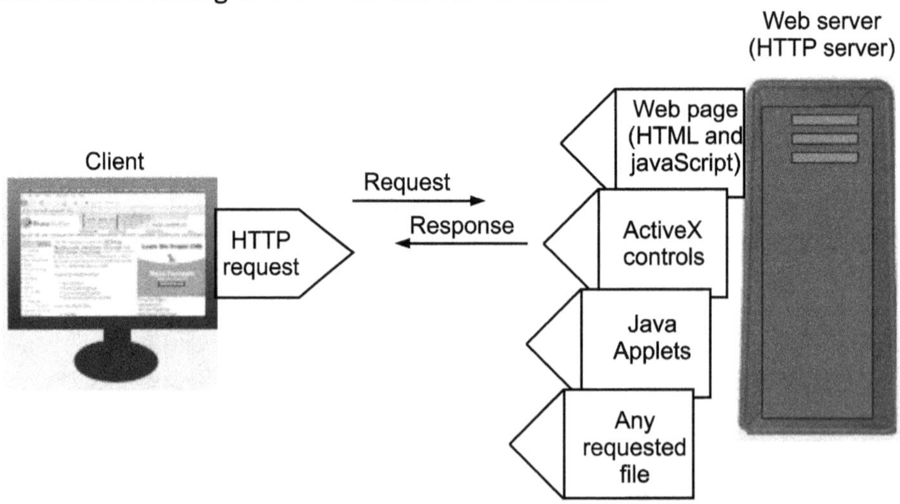

Fig. 1.11: WWW Client-Server Model

1.6 HTTP MESSAGE [S-17, W-17]

- HTTP client and server communicate by sending text messages.
- An HTTP message consists of a message header and an optional message body, separated by a blank line, as shown in Fig. 1.12.

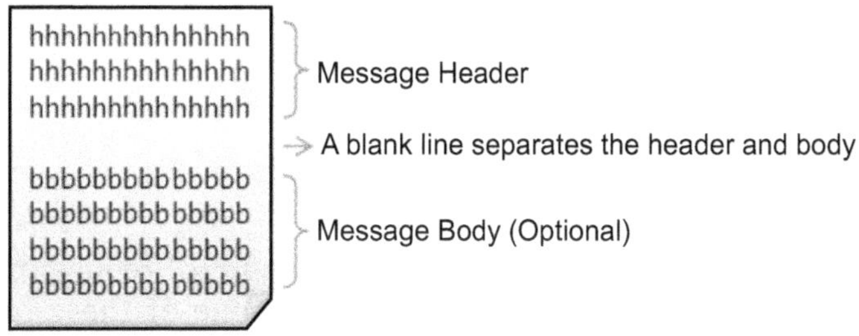

Fig. 1.12: HTTP Message

- The client sends a request message to the server. The server returns a response message, (See Fig. 1.13).

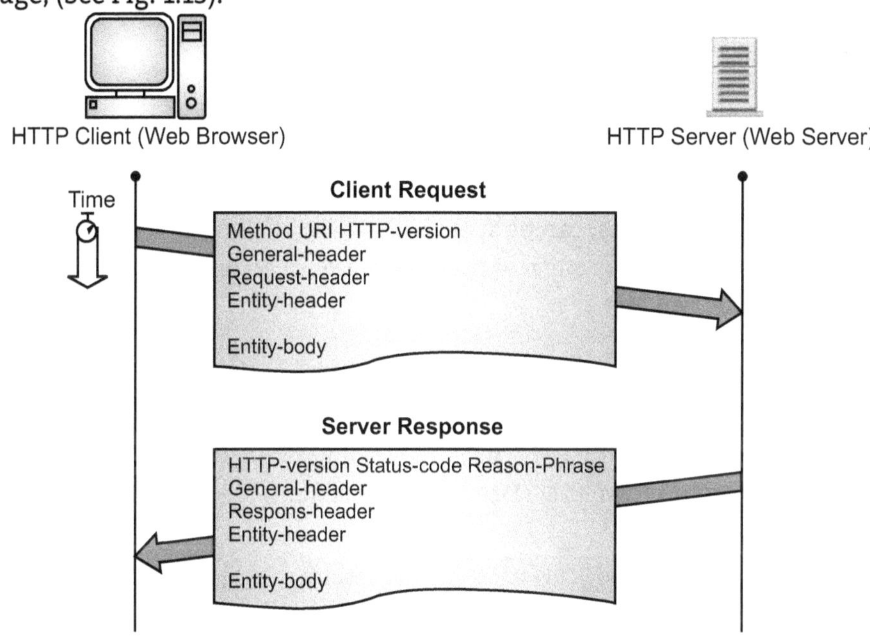

Fig. 1.13: Message transfer in Client-Server

1.6.1 Request Message **[S-19, 16]**

- The formats of the request and response messages are similar; both are shown in Fig. 1.14.

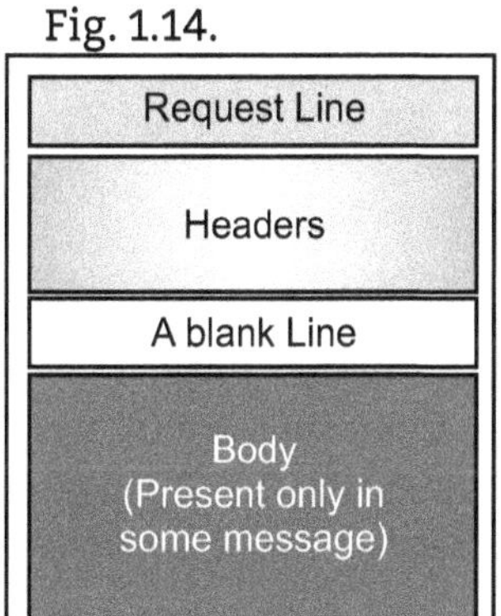

(a) Request message

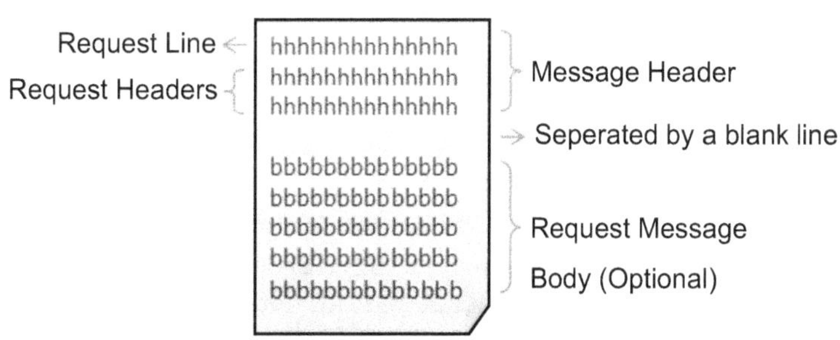

(b) HTTP Request Message

Fig. 1.14: HTTP Request Message

- **Request Line:** The first line of the header is called the request line, followed by optional request headers.
- The request line has the following syntax:

```
request-method-name request-URI HTTP-version
```

where,

  - **request-method-name:** HTTP protocol defines a set of request methods, e.g., GET, POST, HEAD, and OPTIONS. The client can use one of these methods to send a request to the server.
  - **request-URI:** Specifies the resource requested.
  - **HTTP-version:** Two versions are currently in use: HTTP/1.0 and HTTP/1.1.
- Examples of request line are:

```
GET /test.html HTTP/1.1
HEAD /query.html HTTP/1.0
POST /index.html HTTP/1.1
```

- **Request Headers:** The request headers are in the form of name:value pairs. Multiple values, separated by commas, can be specified.

```
request-header-name: request-header-value1, request-header-value2, ...
```

Examples of request headers are:

```
Host: www.xyz.com
Connection: Keep-Alive
Accept: image/gif, image/jpeg, */*
Accept-Language: us-en, fr, cn
```

- Fig. 1.15 shows an example of a HTTP request message.

Example:

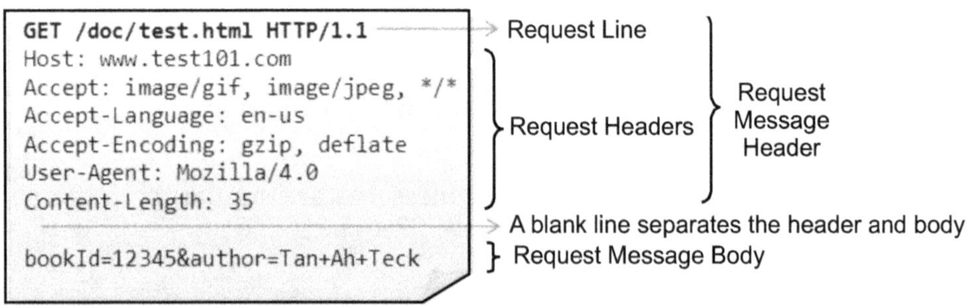

Fig. 1.15: Example for Request Message

HTTP Request Methods:

- HTTP protocol defines a set of request methods. A client can use one of these request methods to send a request message to an HTTP server. The methods are:
  1. **GET:** A client can use the GET request to get a web resource from the server.
  2. **HEAD:** A client can use the HEAD request to get the header that a GET request would have obtained. Since the header contains the last-modified date of the data, this can be used to check against the local cache copy.
  3. **POST:** Used to post data up to the web server.
  4. **PUT:** Ask the server to store the data.

5. **DELETE:** Ask the server to delete the data.
6. **TRACE:** Ask the server to return a diagnostic trace of the actions it takes.
7. **OPTIONS:** Ask the server to return the list of request methods it supports.
8. **CONNECT:** Used to tell a proxy to make a connection to another host and simply reply the content, without attempting to parse or cache it. This is often used to make SSL connection through the proxy.

1.6.2 Response Message

- The format of the HTTP response message is shown in Fig. 1.16.

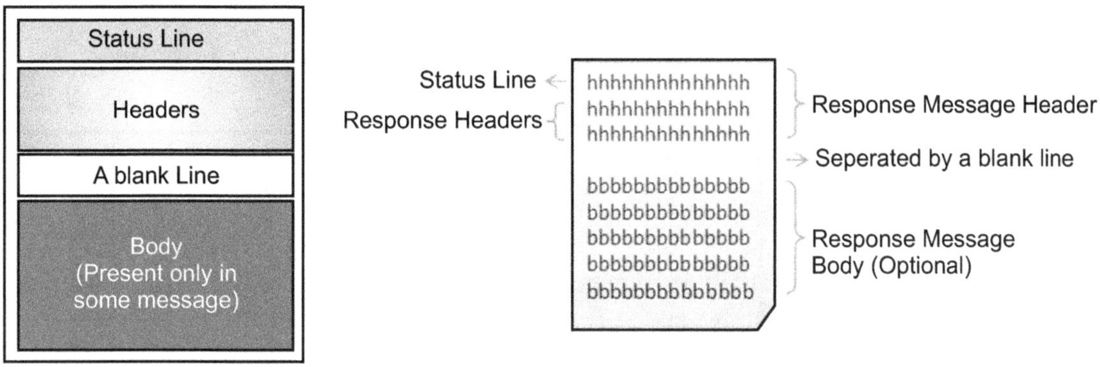

(a) Response message **(b) Response Message**

Fig. 1.16: HTTP Response Mesasge

- **Status Line:** The first line is called the *Status Line*, followed by optional response header(s).
- The status line has the following syntax:

```
HTTP-version status-code reason-phrase
```

where,

  - **HTTP-version:** The HTTP version used in this session. Either HTTP/1.0 and HTTP/1.1.
  - **status-code:** A 3-digit number generated by the server to reflect the outcome of the request.
  - **reason-phrase:** Gives a short explanation to the status code.
  - **Common status code and reason-phrase:** are "200 OK", "404 Not Found", "403 Forbidden", "500 Internal Server Error".
- Examples of status line are:

```
HTTP/1.1 200 OK
HTTP/1.0 404 Not Found
HTTP/1.1 403 Forbidden
```

- **Response Headers:** The response headers are in the form name:value pairs: response-header-name: response-header-value1, response-header-value2, ...
- Examples of response headers are:

```
Content-Type: text/html
Content-Length: 35
Connection: Keep-Alive
Keep-Alive: timeout=15, max=100
```

  - The response message body contains the resource data requested.

- Fig. 1.17 shows example of HTTP response message.

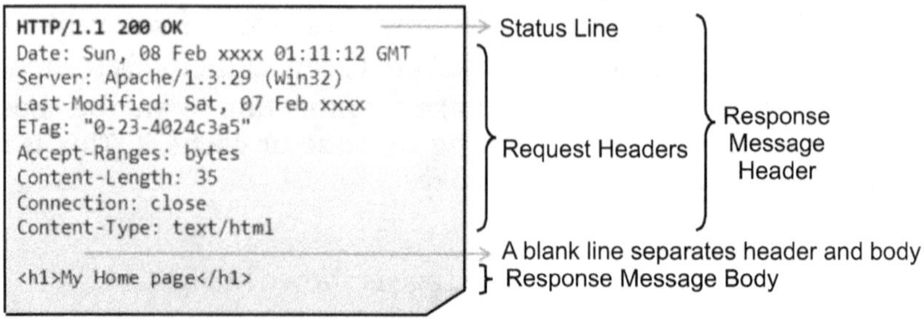

Fig. 1.17: Example HTTP Response Message

Summary

- Web technologies are related to the interface between web servers and their clients. This information includes markup languages, programming interfaces, languages and standards for document identification and display.
- The World Wide Web abbreviated as WWW or W3 and commonly known as the Web. WWW is a system of interlinked hypertext documents accessed via the Internet.
- HTML is the main markup language for displaying web pages and other information that can be displayed in a web browser
- Website is a set of related web pages containing content such as text, images, video, audio, etc.
- A web application or web app is any software that runs in a web browser.
- A web page is a document, typically written in plain text distributed with formatting instructions of HyperText Markup Languages like HTML, XHTML.
- A static web page sometimes called a flat page/stationary page is a web page that is delivered to the user exactly as stored.
- A dynamic web page is a web page with web content that varies based on parameters provided by a user or a computer program.
- Web publishing, or "online publishing," is the process of publishing content on the Internet.
- The web is a collection of files known as web pages. Web pages can contain hyperlinks which point to other web pages.
- A web browser (commonly referred to as a browser) is a software application for retrieving, presenting and traversing information resources on the WWW.
- Client-Server Model is a technology which is based on distribution of task or function between two independent processes i.e. Client and Server.
- The communication in clients and servers exchange messages in a request-response messaging pattern.
- The Internet is a global system of interconnected computer networks that use the standard Internet protocol suite (TCP/IP) to link several billion devices worldwide.
- The HTTP is a protocol that is used to define how the client-server programs can be written to retrieve web pages from the Web.
- The FTP is used to transfer files between two computers over a network and Internet.
- IP is the fundamental building block for all control and data exchanges across and within the Internet.

Check Your Understanding

Multiple Choice Questions.

1. Central Computer which is powerful than other computers in the network is called as ______.
   (a) Client (b) Server
   (c) Hub (d) Switch
2. The applications of the Client and Server Model are ______.
   (a) World Wide Web (b) Network Printing
   (c) E-mail (d) All of the above
3. A client can use the ______ request to get a web resource from the server.
   (a) PUT (b) POST
   (c) GET (d) HEAD
4. The first line of the header is called the ______ followed by optional request headers.
   (a) Status line (b) Request Line
   (c) Headers (d) Body
5. The first line of the header is called the ______ followed by optional response headers.
   (a) Status line (b) Request Line
   (c) Headers (d) Body
6. HTTP is a ______ protocol.
   (a) connectionless (b) connection oriented
   (c) object oriented (d) None of Above
7. The communication in clients and server exchange messages in a ______ messaging pattern.
   (a) request-response (b) response-request
   (c) server-client (d) None of Above

Answers

1. (b)	2. (d)	3. (c)	4. (b)	5. (a)	6. (b)	7. (a)

Practice Questions

Q.1 Answer the following Question in short.

1. What is meant by Web technologies?
2. What is HTTP?
3. List out HTTP request methods.
4. What is use of FTP protocol.
5. What is static web pages.
6. What is dynamic web pages.

Q.2 Answer the following Question in detail.

1. What is static and dynamic web pages?
2. With the help of diagram describe client-server model.
3. Write short note on: communication in client-server.
4. Describe FTP in detail.
5. What is IP? Explain in detail.
6. Define WWW? How it is works?
7. Enlist HTTP messages with example.
8. Write short note on Internet.
9. Write short note on HTTP.
10. Explain request message and response message.

Q.3 Define the following terms.

1. Web page
2. Web application
3. Website

Previous Exams Questions

Summer 2019

1. Write any two HTTP request methods. **[2 M]**

Ans. Refer to Section 1.6.1.

2. Explain Client-server communication. **[4 M]**

Ans. Refer to Section 1.2.

3. Write short note on Internet. **[4 M]**

Ans. Refer to Section 1.3.

Summer 2018

1. Define the term internet protocol. **[2 M]**

Ans. Refer to Section 1.4.

2. Write short note on FTP. **[4 M]**

Ans. Refer to Section 1.4.2.

Winter 2017

1. Write a note on HTTP. **[4 M]**

Ans. Refer to Section 1.4.1.

2. Write short note on Internet. **[4 M]**

Ans. Refer to Section 1.3.

Summer 2017

1. Write a note on HTTP. **[4 M]**

Ans. Refer to Section 1.4.1.

2. Write a note on Internet. **[4 M]**

Ans. Refer to Section 1.3.

Winter 2016

1. Write a short note on WWW and FTP. **[4 M]**

Ans. Refer to Sections 1.5 and 1.4.2.

2. Write a short note on Internet. **[4 M]**

Ans. Refer to Section 1.3.

Summer 2016

1. Give any two http request methods. **[2 M]**

Ans. Refer to Section 1.6.

2. Write a note on FTP. **[4 M]**

Ans. Refer to Section 1.4.2.

3. Explain client-server communication. **[4 M]**

Ans. Refer to Section 1.2.

■■■

2...

Web Design

Objectives...

- ▣ To learn concepts of Effective Web Design.
- ▣ To learn web design issues including Browser Bandwidth and Cache.
- ▣ To learn Display Resolution and Look and Feel of the Website.
- ▣ To learn Page Layout and Linking.
- ▣ To learn User Centric Design and Sitemap.
- ▣ To learn Planning and Publishing Website and Designing Effective Navigation.

2.1 INTRODUCTION

- A website is a collection of web pages which are linked together in a certain fashion. website is written in HTML and hosted on web server.
- Each website is provided with a unique Uniform Resource Locator (URL). It is accessed and transported through the HyperText Transfer Protocol (HTTP).
- Website design requires many different skills and disciplines in the production and maintenance of websites.
- Website designer not only think about the content of the website but also think about its look.

2.2 CONCEPTS OF EFFECTIVE WEB DESIGN

- Website designer design a website strictly according to the user's requirements. Quality of website is also important factor.
- There are various factors where performance of the website depends like content, accessibility, global presence, hyperlinks, human computer interface, attractiveness, visual style, objective, color combination, graphics, fonts, convey information, page layout, texts, paragraph formatting, images, lists, icons, navigation, updated information, page loading speed, security, etc. if these parameters are handled carefully then the quality websites can be produced.
- Following are some concepts about web page designing which will help us to design an effective web page:
  - Website design is affected by various environmental issues such as browser support, bandwidth of the connection, cache support and display resolution of the monitor.
  - Look and feel also determines the overall appearance of the website to a greater extent.

- The website theme, fonts, graphics and colors need to be carefully chosen.
- The presentation of information should be clear and easy to access.
- Page templates are used to design individual pages using grid structure and distribute the content for quick view and easy access.
- Design of the website is to be done after considering various user requirements and choices to make it user centric.
- Website planning is most important activity to prepare an effective website design.
- Navigation is the most important design element that makes website clear, consistent, meaningful and understandable.

2.3 WEB DESIGN ISSUES INCLUDING BROWSER BANDWIDTH AND CACHE

- A browser is an application software which is used to display web pages. e.g. Firefox, Internet explorer, Opera, Chrome etc. Browser runs on client machines.
- When user wants some web page from server then he makes the request for it using web browser. Then the requested web page comes from the server to client and displayed by the web browser.
- The web page is written in HTML which is interpreted by the web browser and display according to content.
- Web browser supports JPEG, PNG, GIF images, and PDF.
- The common web design issues are: the web pages must be portable on different browser, attractive in terms of color and graphics, rich in contents, easy to read and navigate and download faster.
- Different browser interprets same HTML tag in different way. Similarly, different HTML tags are supported by different browsers and their versions. The older versions of a browser may not support recent HTML tags and features.
- Web pages are not portable on different browsers and different versions of browser. So browser compatibility is a serious issue.
- To make web page portable, it is tested on different browser on different operating system and use development tools to add special features supported by majority web browsers. The best way to avoid these problems is to follow the standard and use the validation rule recommended by W3C.

Bandwidth and Cache:

- Users have different connection speed, i.e. bandwidth. While designing the web page, the connection speed should also be considered, because connection speed plays an important role to access the websites.
- If user has low bandwidth connection and a web page contains too many images, it takes more time to download. Hence while designing web pages; we have to consider the users who have low bandwidth or speed.
- Also we have to limit the number of images in a single web page so that the downloading can be faster.

- In common language, caching means placing some data in memory. So that, when the same data is needed next time, it could be directly retrieved from the memory.
- When we visit a website, our browser takes pieces of the page and stores them on our computer's hard drive.
- Some of the assets our browser will stores Images - logos, pictures, backgrounds, etc., HTML, CSS, and JavaScript. Browsers typically cache the static assets i.e. parts of a website that do not change from visit to visit.
- What to cache and for how long is determined by the website designer. Some assets are removed from our machine in a few days while others may remain in our cache for up to a year.
- When the user gives the URL of the web page for the first time, HTML file together with all graphics files referred in a page is downloaded and displayed. At the same time, the images downloaded are also stored in cache area of browser for specified time as per user's preference.
- When the next time the same page is visited, the browser gets only HTML file and uses the images from the cache which increases the download speed.

2.4 DISPLAY RESOLUTION

- The size and quality of computer screen is called as Display Resolution or Screen Resolution.
- Screen resolutions are indicated by a set of two numbers such as 1024×768 – a screen with this resolution can display 1,024 distinct dots (or pixels) on each of 768 lines, which are about 780,000 pixels. The more pixels we are able to display the more visual real estate we have on our screen.
- Display resolution is another important factor which affects the web page design; because we do not have any control on display resolution of the monitors on which user views our pages.
- Today, most monitors are using resolution of 1024×768 pixels. However, many old monitors are working on 800×600. Considering the different resolutions, we have three choices for web design.
  - Design a web page with fixed resolution. In this case if web page resolution is 800×600 then the web page properly fits into a screen, but leaves some part of the screen if resolutions screen is 1024×768. On the other side, if design is fixed to use 1024×768 pixels, it will not fit into the screen having 800×600 resolutions.
  - Make a flexible design using HTML table to fit into different resolutions. In this case the web page is divided into three columns with the middle column having a variable width. Depending on the resolution of monitor on which page is viewed, it change its width.
  - If the page is displayed on a monitor with a higher resolution, the page is displayed on left-hand side and some part on the right-hand side remain blanks. We can use centred design to display page, e.g. in middle of the screen, leaving equal space on both the side of the page.

2.5 LOOK AND FEEL OF THE WEBSITE

- Look and Feel of the websites decides the overall appearance of the website. "Look and Feel" is how the site looks to the user and how it feels when user is interacting with it.
- The "Look" is defined by the following components of our website:
  - Websites themes.
  - Web typography.
  - Graphics.
  - Color palette.
  - Layout.
  - Font styles and choices.
  - Overall styling and spacing.
  - Visual structure.
  - Navigation.
- The "Feel" is determined by the following characteristics:
  - The movement and response of dynamic components like dropdown menus, buttons, forms, and galleries.
  - Sound effects.
  - The speed by which pages and images load.

2.5.1 Major Look and Feel Components of Website

1. Website Theme:

- Website theme focuses on the unification of design that should be reflected in each element of the design such that all pages of the website hold together and give the impression of a single unit.
- Consider the following points while designing the website theme:
  - Use logo of the company in the theme. In this case, the logo must appear on each page to convey a message.
  - Use color scheme in the theme. In this case, all buttons, link, titles, labels and other text should use it consistently.
  - Website for global warming can use pictures, message related to cause and effects of the global warming on live.

2. Fonts:

- Consider the following points while choosing the typefaces for websites.
  - Different fonts have different readability and it directly affects the user psychology. Some fonts are good to continuous reading while others for viewing from distance such as advertisement on hoardings.
  - Remember that height and width of the same character is different in different font. This affects the line endings and paragraph boundaries.
  - Maintain consistency while using the font type and size. Don't use too many fonts with too large sizes. Select few fonts only and use them with different sizes and modes (bold, italic, underline) for headers (main and sub-headers), title and text. Use of CSS helps in maintaining consistency.

- Consider the availability of fonts on visitor's machine. If the font used in web page is not installed on visitor's machine, browser uses default font, Time New Roman.

3. Color:

- Consider the following points while choosing the color for websites.
  - Use the same color palette.
  - Pick two or three base colors at most for our design, and then use tints (which are lighter, mixed with white) and shades (which are darker, mixed with black) of these base colors to expand the palette where necessary.
  - Color can help convey a mood or a feeling. e.g.
    - If the mood should be trustworthy, the user should get a sense that the company has strength. The designer might use a darker shade of blue. Blue can also be used to convey the mood such as spiritual or symbolize peace.
    - The color red for some can mean passion or love. But it can also mean stop or danger for others. Use the color red wisely.
    - If the mood should be happy, orange color may be used because the orange color is associated with joy and sunshine. Orange color will also convey a sense of energy, passion, stimulation and encouragement.
  - Color Pallet of 3 to 5 colors is created and to be used throughout the website for text, buttons, icons, links, and forms to keep the look and feel uniform and non-cluttered.

4. Graphics:

- Graphics make the website attractive and convey lots of information. Graphics include images, charts and many others. Consider the following points while using graphics:
  - One of the important points is the graphics file format. Popular image formats on web are JPG, GIF, PNG, etc. Use them at right place considering their features. Different file formats support different features and levels of compression.
  - Too many graphics or images with larger sizes reduce the download speed. Use limited graphics or use images with smaller size or in compressed format.
  - Use images that suit the theme of the website and profile of target audience rather using any image just to include graphics.

5. Presentation and Access:

- Websites are viewed by the peoples having different reading habits and expectations. So, the presentation must be clear so that, the desired information can be accessed quickly and easily without any hurdles. Consider the following points:
  - Web page should be divided in visually different areas to present the contents with different important. Use grid-based structures to divide the web pages into different rows and columns.
  - Make different parts of the pages area visible by using the white space, i.e. the blank areas between them to make the contents eye-catching.
  - Keep the page simple and focused.

- Do not overload a page with too much content. Divide the contents into parts, i.e. sections within sections and link them using hyperlink.
- Don't make page too lengthy. Instead divide it, into multiple pages with link such as "previous" and "next" to move forward and backward.
- If a long page is to be designed, provide the link to top of the page at the bottom to quickly return to start.
- Links between the pages and sections should exhibit consistency in appearance and meaning otherwise, that make navigation difficult for the visitors.
- Navigations, i.e. transitions between pages, should reflect the consistency in terms of graphics for links and their placement. In this put the common links at the same place on each page.

2.6 PAGE LAYOUT AND LINKING

- Website consists of individual web pages that are linked together using various links. Page layout defines the visual structure of the page. In this structure the page area is divided into different parts to present the information like text, images, graphics, videos etc.
- Page layout allows the designer to distribute the contents in a page such that visitor can view it easily and find necessary details.
- The page layout contains the following things:
  - **Header:** This is the top section of the page which displays the site logo, name, slogan and often the main menu.
  - **Main Content:** The section of the page where we insert and manage content. This section fits prominently in the middle of the page.
  - **Sidebar Left/Right:** The columns on the left and right side of the main content section is called as sidebar. Within these sidebars sections are called blocks; these blocks can display secondary menus, pictures, etc.
  - **Footer:** This is the bottom section of the page which displays the text about copyright or credits and other links.
- While distributing the content in layout, balance should be made between text and graphics. Too much graphics may slow down the page.
- Once the page layouts are prepared, we have to link them together to provide the navigation paths consistently so that the user can find the desired information quickly and easily.

2.7 USER CENTRIC DESIGN

- It is very difficult for web designer to predict the exact behaviour of the website user.
- However, idea about behaviour of common user helps in making design of the website user centric.
- Users either scan the information on the web page to find the section of their interest or read the information to get the details. If the information is provided for reading, e.g. article of an online magazine or news paper site, then user's general reading habit

gives the idea of how to organize such information. People normally read from left-to-right and top-to bottom. Hence we can organize such contents in column fashion on a web page.

- The link in table of contents change colors once visited, so user get an idea of which link have been visited and which are yet to be visited.

2.8 SITEMAP

- Many times websites are too complex as there are a large number of sections and each section contain many pages. It becomes difficult for a visitor to quickly move from one part to another. Once the user selects a particular section and pages in that section, the user get confused about where he/she is and where to go from there.
- To make it simple, keep our hierarchy of information to few levels or to provide the navigation bar on each page to jump directly to a particular section.
- Another solution is to provide the sitemap including links to each section and their pages directly sitemap gives the organisation of contents of a website graphically.
- The following figure shows sitemap:

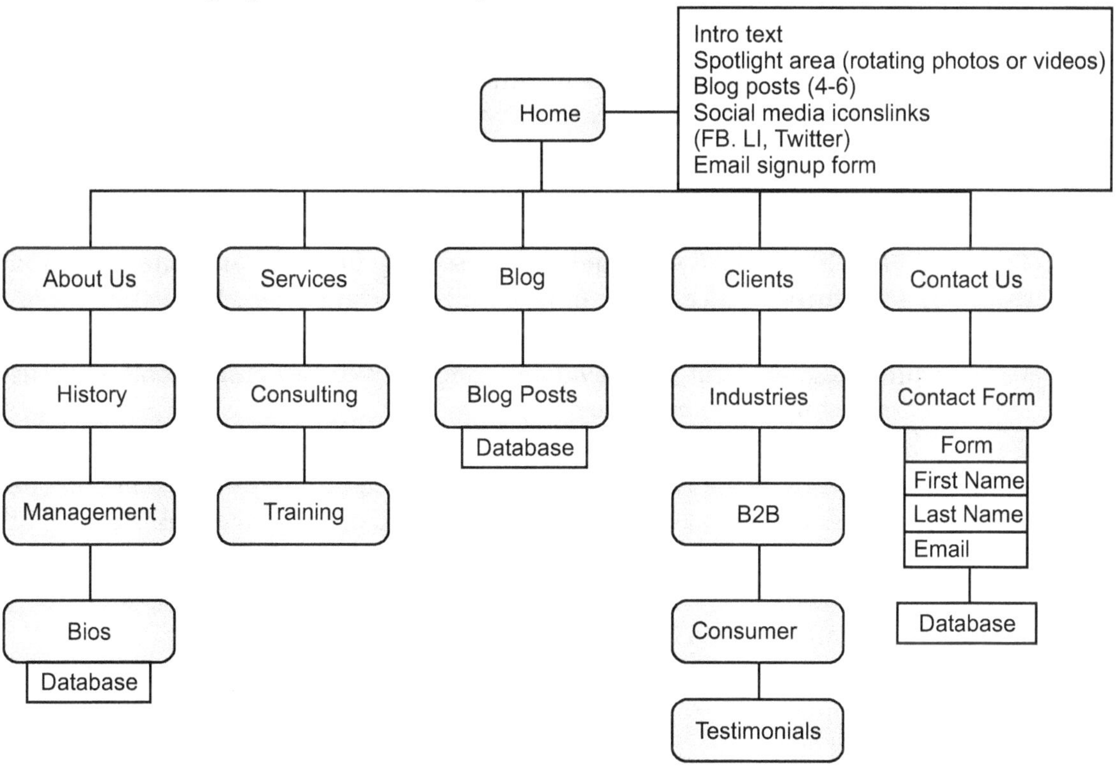

Fig. 2.1: Sitemap

2.9 PLANNING AND PUBLISHING WEBSITE

2.9.1 Website Planning

- The most important activity in a website development is planning. To achieve higher success of the website in terms of user satisfaction, better planning is needed.

- The basic steps that help in planning a website are:
  - **Define Target Audience:** First find out who are the visitors of the website so that according to the visitors the information can be organized like font, color, images etc. The following points can be consider while defining target audience:
    - The viewer's background and previous experience.
    - Their interest and tastes.
    - The reason why they are visiting our site.
    - What is their general age.
  - **Organize Concepts and Materials:** The aim of creating website should be clear. Whether the aim of the site is:
    - To inform.
    - To promote a product.
    - To educate audience.
    - To entertain the audience

    Vision of creating the website needs to be well defined. Once the goals are defined, organize all the information such as text, font, color, images etc. accordingly.
  - **Create a Directory structure:** If the website contain very few files then that files can be stored in just one directory. But if the site is going to be very large and complex, then the files need to organized into separate directories and sub-directories. Developing a logical directory structure is an essential part of planning our website. We can have a subdirectory for sound clippings.
  - **Create a Sketch of the web pages:** After setting up a general site plan and directory structures, the contents may fall into certain types. With the help of these a sketch of the web page can be created.

    Various pre-designed templates available on the web designing tools such as Macromedia Dreamweaver can also be used.
  - **Develop a Look and Feel:** The term Look and Feel means the overall representation of website. It is the combination of color, graphics, type and text etc. The following factors can be taken into consideration to improve the look and feel of the website:
    - **Space and Balance:** Every thing should look proportionate and proper.
    - **Color:** The colors should look pleasant to the eyes.
    - **Font type and size:** Type face of the text and size of the text in the web pages should be comfortable to read and make the matter easy to understand.
    - **Textures:** Background graphics or textures can not be irritating while reading text.
    - **Special Effects:** Multimedia can be added to make site appealing. More animation, graphics, sound may cause delay while accessing through a browser.
    - **Consistency:** Using a single color scheme throughout is a good way to achieve consistency.

2.9.2 Website Publishing

- Once website is designed and developed, the next step is to publish it so that website is available for everyone.
- Web publishing is the process of publishing content on the Internet. It includes creating and uploading websites, updating web pages, and posting blogs online. The websites are uploaded on the remote server. The clients which are connected to the server can see the website. The published content may include text, images, videos etc.
- In order to publish content on the web, we need three things:
  - **Web development software:** The software may be a professional web design program like Dreamweaver or a simple web-based interface like WordPress.
  - **Internet connection:** Internet connection is used to upload the content to the web server.
  - **Web server:** Large sites may use a dedicated web host, but many smaller sites often reside on shared servers, which host multiple websites. Most blogs are published on public web servers through a free service like Blogger.

2.10 DESIGNING EFFECTIVE NAVIGATION

- Navigation means the way to move from one page to another page in website. To move from one page to another page, hyperlinks are used. If navigation design is not proper then the visitor of the site may feels problems.
- Following are some points for effective navigation:
  - Links are either text based or graphical.
  - Link should be clear and meaningful.
  - For all the web pages the links text or graphics must be same.
  - Link must be understandable. Link itself guides the user about content.
  - Links belongs to same type of contains can be group together.
  - Provide search link if necessary at the top of the page.
  - Provide link for Home Page.
  - Provide navigation menu on the left sidebar to directly move to a particular section.
  - Horizontal menu bar is used to directly jump to any section from anywhere.

Summary

- Website design requires many different skills and disciplines in the production and maintenance of websites.
- There are various factors where performance of the website depends like content, hyperlinks, attractiveness, visual style, objective, color combination, graphics, fonts, page layout, texts, images, navigation, updated information, page loading speed, security, etc.
- Website design is affected by various environmental issues such as browser support, bandwidth of the connection, cache support and display resolution of the monitor.
- Web pages are not portable on different browsers and different versions of browser.

- The best way to avoid these problems is to follow the standard and use the validation rule recommended by W3C.
- Users have different connection speed, i.e. bandwidth.
- Limit the number of images in a single web page so that the downloading can be faster.
- The images downloaded are stored in cache area of browser. When the next time the same page is visited, the browser gets only HTML file and uses the images from the cache which increases the download speed significantly.
- The size and quality of computer screen is called as Display Resolution or Screen Resolution, which are indicated by a set of two numbers such as 1024×768.
- Look and Feel of the websites decides the overall appearance of the website.
- Website theme focuses on the unification of design that should be reflected in each element of the design such that all pages of the website hold together and give the impression of a single unit.
- Maintain consistency while using the font type and size. Select few fonts only and use them with different sizes and modes (bold, italic, underline) for headers (main and sub-headers), title and text. Use of CSS helps in maintaining consistency.
- Page layout defines the visual structure of the page. Which contains: Header, Main Content, Sidebar Left/Right, and Footer.
- Once the page layouts are prepared, we have to link them together to provide the navigation paths consistently so that the user can find the desired information quickly and easily.
- Provide the sitemap including links to each section and their pages, it gives the organisation of contents of a website graphically.
- To achieve higher success of the website in terms of user satisfaction, better planning is needed.
- Navigation means the way to move from one page to another page in website.
- Web publishing is the process of publishing content on the Internet.
- The term WWW refers to the World Wide Web or simply the Web.

Check Your Understanding

Multiple Choice Questions.

1. Which of the following is used to create a web page?
   (a) HTML (b) HTTP
   (c) XML (d) JVM
2. Which of the following software could be used to build a website?
   (a) Power Point (b) Excel
   (c) Dreamweaver (d) ERP
3. Which of the following statement is true?
   (a) The web designer should not just be concerned about the looks but also about content.
   (b) Planning is very important in web design.
   (c) Both a and b.
   (d) None of the above.

4. A good rule of thumb is to limit each website to no more than ____ font variations.
   (a) One (b) Two
   (c) Three (d) Four
5. Downloading speed can be increase by ____
   (a) Decreasing the bandwidth
   (b) Limiting the number of images in a web page
   (c) Choosing the right font
   (d) None of the above
6. Different web pages of a website are linked together using ____
   (a) Color palette (b) Links
   (c) Themes (d) Typography
7. Which of the following point is considered as good designing?
   (a) All buttons, link, titles, labels and other text should be use consistently.
   (b) Use too many graphics or large sized images.
   (c) Use different color palette for different pages.
   (d) Use too many large size fonts.
8. Websites are uploaded ____
   (a) To the client machine (b) To the server machine
   (c) Both a and b (d) Protocol
9. Which of the following statement is false?
   (a) Screen resolutions are indicated by a set of two numbers.
   (b) Different browser interprets same HTML tag in different way.
   (c) Each website is provided with a unique uniform resource locator.
   (d) Browsers typically cache the dynamic assets.
10. Which of the following statement is false?
   (a) Using a single color scheme throughout is not a good way to achieve consistency.
   (b) The web pages must be portable on different browser.
   (c) Users have different bandwidth.
   (d) Sitemap gives the organisation of contents of a website graphically.

Answers

1. (a)	2. (c)	3. (c)	4. (c)	5. (b)	6. (b)	7. (a)	8. (b)	9. (d)	10. (a)

Practice Questions

Q.1 Answer the following Question in short.

1. What are two common ways in which we can increase the download speed of a website?
2. What are the two ways to avoid problems related with browser portability?
3. Enlist different look and feel components of website.

4. Write any four factors which can be considered to improve the look and feel of the website.
5. What are the three things are needed to publish a website on the web?
6. What are the different factors of designing effective navigation?

Q.2 Answer the following Question in detail.

1. Explain concepts of effective web design in details.
2. Write short notes on browser compatibility.
3. Explain the working of caching.
4. What are the different points to be considered while designing the website theme?
5. What are the different points to be considered while choosing the typefaces for websites?
6. What are the different points to be considered while choosing the color for websites?
7. What are the different points to be considered while using graphics for website?
8. What are the different points to be considered while designing the layout of website?
9. Explain in brief the different contents of page layout of a website.
10. Describe the importance of sitemap in website.
11. Describe the basic steps that help in planning a website.

Q.3 Define the following terms.

1. Bandwidth.
2. Display resolution.
3. Website theme.
4. Web publishing.
5. Navigation.

■■■

3... HTML

Objectives...

- To understand introduction to HTML.
- To study basic HTML structure and common HTML tags.
- To learn physical and logical HTML.
- To study types of images, client side and server side image mapping.
- To learn List, Table, Frames, Embedding Audio, Video.
- To study HTML Form and Form elements.

3.1 INTRODUCTION TO HTML

- HyperText Markup Language (HTML), is the standard markup language used to create web pages.
- HTML stands for HyperText Markup Language.
- An HTML file is a text file containing small markup tags. The markup tags tell the web browser how to display the page.
- An HTML file can be created using a simple text editor.
- HTML was invented in 1990 by a scientist called Tim Berners-Lee.
- Hypertext refers to the way in which web pages (HTML documents) are linked together. When we click a link in a web page, we are using hypertext.
- Markup language describes how HTML works. With a markup language, we simply "mark up" a text document with tags that tell a web browser how to structure it to display. A markup language is a set of markup tags and the tags describes document content.

3.2 BASIC HTML STRUCTURE [W-16, 17]

- A web page is also known as HTML page or HTML document. Fig. 3.1 shows page structure of HTML.
- HTML files are text files featuring semantically tagged elements.
- HTML filenames are suffixed with .htm or .html extensions.

- A web page is marked by an opening <html>tag and a closing </html> tag and is divided into the following three major sections:
  1. **Comment Section (optional):** This section contains comments about the web page. It is important to include comments that tell us that is going on in the web page.
  2. **Head Section (optional):** The head section is defined with a starting <head> tag and closing </head> tag. This section usually contains a title for the web page as shown in the Fig. 3.1.
  3. **Body Section:** The body section comes after the head section. The body section contains the entire information about the web page and its behaviour.
- A web page outline containing these three sections and the opening and closing HTML tags is illustrated in Fig. 3.1.

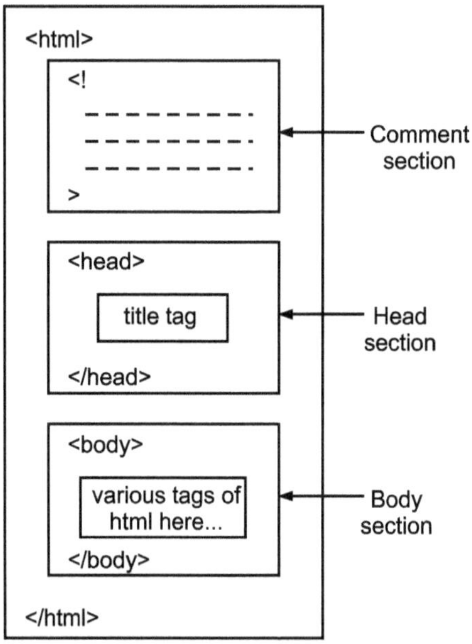

Fig. 3.1: Web page template

HTML Elements:

- HTML elements are the fundamentals of HTML.
- HTML documents are simply a text file made up of HTML elements and these elements are defined using HTML tags. A complete tag, having an opening <tag> and a closing </tag>.
- Every tag in HTML contains some attributes, which provide additional information about HTML elements. Attributes provide additional information about an element.
- Attributes are always specified in the start tag and come in name/value pairs like: name="value".
- HTML element has three basic parts i.e., opening tag, element content and closing tag.

3.2.1 Creating HTML Document

- Creating an HTML document is easy. To begin coding HTML we need only two things: a simple-text editor and a web browser.
- Notepad is the most basic of simple-text editors and we will probably code a fair amount of HTML with it.
- Here are the simple steps to create a basic HTML document:
  1. Open Notepad or another text editor.
  2. At the top of the page type <html>.
  3. On the next line, indent five spaces and now add the opening header tag: <head>.
  4. On the next line, indent ten spaces and type <title> </title>.
  5. Go to the next line, indent five spaces from the margin and insert the closing header tag: </head>.
  6. Five spaces in from the margin on the next line, type<body>.
  7. Now drop down another line and type the closing tag right below the matter: </body>.
  8. Finally, go to the next line and type </html>.
  9. In the File menu, choose Save As.
  10. In the Save as type option box, choose All Files.
  11. Name the file template.htm.
  12. Click Save with .htm or .html extension.

Example for creating a html document.

```
<!DOCTYPE html>
<html>
<head>
<title>
</title>
<body>
    <h1>Nirali Prakashan</h1>
    <p>Textbook Publication Firm.</p>
</body>
</head>
</html>
```

Output:

Nirali Prakashan

Textbook Publication Firm.

- In above example or program:
  - The DOCTYPE declaration defines the document type. The <!DOCTYPE> declaration helps the browser to display a web page correctly.
  - The text between <html> and </html> describes the web page.
  - The text between <body> and </body> is the visible page content.
  - The text between <h1> and </h1> is displayed as a heading.
  - The text between <p> and </p> is displayed as a paragraph contents.

3.3 HTML TAGS [S-18]

- Tags are the instructions that are embedded directly into the text of the document.
- By convention all HTML tags begin with an open angle bracket (<) and end with a close angle bracket (>).
- **Syntax of tag:** `<tag_name> content... </tag_name>`
- HTML tags tells, our browser which elements to present and how to present them. Where the element appears is determined by the order in which the tags appear.

3.3.1 Common HTML Tags

1. **HTML <!DOCTYPE> tag:**

- The HTML <!DOCTYPE> tag is used for specifying which language and version the document is using. This is referred to as the Document Type Declaration (DTD).
- In HTML5, the <!DOCTYPE> declaration is much simpler than in previous versions of HTML, like this:

```
<!DOCTYPE html>
```

- The <!DOCTYPE> declaration must go right at the top of the page, before any other HTML code.

2. **<html> Tag:**

- The <html> tag represents the root of an HTML document.
- The <html> tag is the container that contains all other HTML elements (except for the <!doctype> tag which is located before the opening HTML tag).
- All other HTML elements are nested between the <html> and </html> tags.
- The <html> tag tells the browser that this is an HTML document.

Syntax: `<html>............</html>`

Attribute	Description
1. Manifest	This attribute specifies the address of the document's application cache manifest and the value must be a valid URL.

3. **<title> Tag:**

- The <title> tag is used for declaring the title or name of the HTML document.
- The title is usually displayed in the browser's title bar (at the top) or the <title> tag defines a title in the browser toolbar. It is also displayed in browser bookmarks and search results.

- The title tag is placed between the opening and closing <head> tags.

  Syntax: `<title>..........................</title>`

4. <head> Tag:

- The <head> tag is used for indicating the head section of the HTML document.
- The <head> tag is a container for all the head elements and must include a title for the document, and can include scripts, styles, meta information, and so on.

Example for common HTML tags.

```
<!DOCTYPE html>
<html>
<head>What is meant by Web Technologies?
<title>Web Technologies</title>
<body>
<p>Web technologies related to the interface between web servers and their clients. This information includes markup languages, programming interfaces and languages, and standards for document identification and display.</p>
<p>Parts of Web Technologies:<br>
1. HyperText Markup Language (HTML) is the main markup language for displaying web pages and other information that can be displayed in a web browser.<br>
2. Cascading Style Sheets (CSS) is a style sheet language used for describing the presentation semantics (the look and formatting) of a document written in a markup language.<br>
3. JavaScript (JS) is an open source client-side scripting language commonly implemented as part of a web browser in order to create enhanced user interfaces and dynamic websites.</p>
</body>
</head>
</html>
```

Output:

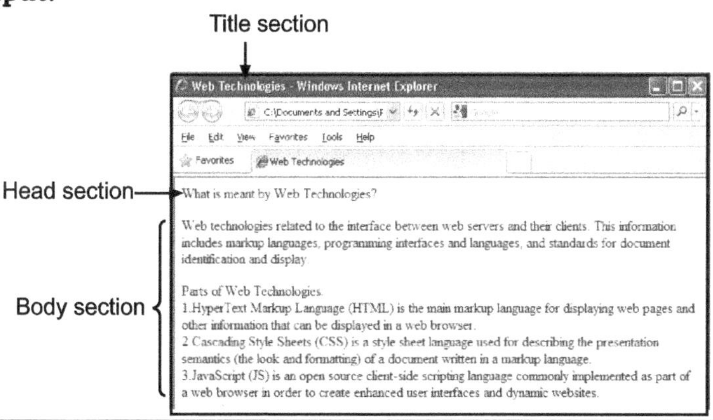

5. <body> Tag:

- The <body> tag defines the document's body.
- The <body> tag is used for indicating the main content section of the HTML document. The body tag is placed between the </head> and the </html> tags.
- The <body> tags contains all the contents of an HTML document, such as text, hyperlinks, images, tables, lists, etc.

  Syntax: `<body>..................</body>`

- Attributes of <body> tag:

Attribute	Value	Description
1. alink	color	This attribute used to specifies the color of an active link in a document
2. background	URL	This attribute used to specifies a background image for a document
3. bgcolor	color	This attribute used to specifies the background color of a document
4. link	color	This attribute used to specifies the color of unvisited links in a document
5. text	color	This attribute used to specifies the color of the text in a document
6. vlink	color	This attribute used to specifies the color of visited links in a document

Example for use of <body> tag.

```
<!DOCTYPE html>
<html>
<head>
<title>HTML <body> tag</title>
<body style="background-color:orange">
<p>Document content goes... here.</p>
</body>
</head>
</html>
```

Output:

3.3.2 Text Formatting Tags [S-17, 16]

- The HTML tags are used for formatting text are called as text formatting tags.
- Following are the text formatting tags used in HTML.

1. <b>	<b> tag defines bold text. Anything that appears in a <b>...</b> element is displayed in bold. **Syntax:** `<b>......</b>`
2. <em>	The <em> tag is used for indicating emphasis. The <em> tag surrounds the word/term being emphasised. **Syntax:** `<em>......</em>`
3. <i>	The content of the <i> tag is usually displayed in italic. The <i> tag can be used to indicate a technical term, a phrase from another language, a thought, or a ship name, etc. **Syntax:** `<i>......</i>`
4. <small>	The <small> tag defines smaller text (and other side comments). The content of the <small> element is displayed one font size smaller than the rest of the text surrounding it. **Syntax:** `<small>......</small>`
5. <strong>	The <strong> tag is used for indicating strong importance for its contents. The strong tag surrounds the emphasized word/phrase. **Syntax:** `<strong>......</strong>`
6. <sub>	The <sub> tag defines subscript text. Subscript text appears half a character below the baseline. Subscript text can be used for chemical formulas, like H_2O. **Syntax:** `<sub>......</sub>`
7. <sup>	The <sup> tag defines superscript text. Superscript text appears half a character above the baseline like 10^5. **Syntax:** `<sup>......</sup>`
8. <ins>	The <ins> tag defines a text that has been inserted into a document. **Syntax:** `<ins>......</ins>`
9. <del>	The <del> tag defines text that has been deleted from a document. **Syntax:** `<del>......</del>`
10. <u>	The <u> tag usually results in the text being underlined. Anything that appears in a <u>...</u> element is displayed with underline, **Syntax:** `<u>......</u>`
11. <strike>	Anything that appears in a <strike> tag is displayed with strikethrough, which is a thin line through the text like, ~~strikethrough.~~ **Syntax:** `<strike>......</strike>`
12. <big>	The content of the <big> element is displayed one font size larger than the rest of the text surrounding it. **Syntax:** `<big>......</big>`

Example for text formatting tags.

```
<!DOCTYPE html>
<head>
<title> HTML <i> <b> <u> example</title>
</head>
<body>
<p>Nirali Prakashan</p>
    <font size="4">Wecome to <b>Nirali Prakashan.</b> <br/></font>
    <font size="2"><i>Nirali Prakashan</i> is a textbook publication
    firm.<br/></font>
    <font face="verdana" color="black">Nirali Prakashan <u>publised more
    than 3500 book titles.</u></font>
</body>
</html>
```

Output:

Nirali Prakashan

Wecome to **Nirali Prakashan.**
Nirali Prakashan is a textbook publication firm.
Nirali Prakashan <u>publised more than 3500 book titles.</u>

Example for subscript and superscript tags.

```
<!DOCTYPE html>
<head>
<title> HTML <sub> <sup> example</title>
</head>
<body>
<h3> Mathematical Formula</h3>
<p>2<sup>10</sup>+ LOG<sub>10</sup><sup>5</sup></p>
</body>
</html>
```

Output:

Mathematical Formula

2^{10}+ $LOG_{10}{}^{5}$

3.3.3 HTML "Computer Output" Tags [W-17, S-19, 17]

- Following table shows various types of computer output tags.

Tag	Description
1. <pre>	The HTML <pre> tag is used for indicating preformatted text. The code tag surrounds the code being marked up. Browsers normally render <pre> text in a fixed-pitched font, with whitespace and without word wrap. **Syntax:** `<pre>.........</pre>`

Example for <pre>tag.

```
<!DOCTYPE html>
<head>
<title>HTML <pre> tag Example</title>
<body>
<pre>This text has been formatted using the HTML pre tag. The brower should
   display all white space as it was entered.
</pre>
<pre width="30">
   Text in a pre tag is displayed in a fixed-width font, and it preserves
   both spaces and line breaks
</pre>
</body>
</head>
</html>
```

Output:

```
This text has
been formatted using
   the HTML pre tag. The brower should
      display all white space
as it was entered.

Text in a pre tag is d i s p l a y e d in a f i x e d - w i d t h
font, and it preserves both     spaces    and
line breaks
```

3.3.4 Block Level Tags

- Most HTML elements are defined as block level elements or as inline elements.
- Block level elements normally start (and end) with a new line when displayed in a browser.

(i) <!--...--> comment Tag:

- The comment tag is used to insert comments in the source code.
- Comments are not displayed in the browsers.
- Comments can be inserted into the HTML code to make it more readable and understandable. Comments are ignored by the browser and are not displayed.

Example for comment tag.

```
<html>
<title> HTML comment </title>
<!-- The level 4 heading goes here -->
<h4>How to comment out your code.</h4>
<h3>!--.....-- tag used for comment and they are simply there for the
programmer's benefit.</h3>
<!-- The text goes here -->
<p>This code demonstrates the HTML code to hide your comments.</p>
</html>
```

Output:

How to comment out your code.

!--....-- tag used for comment and they are simply there for the programmer's benefit.

This code demonstrates the HTML code to hide your comments.

(ii) HTML heading tags:

- The HTML <h1> to <h6> tags are used to define HTML headings. <h1> defines the most important heading. While <h6> defines the least important heading.

  Syntax:

```
<h1>...........</h1>
<h2>...........</h2>
<h3>...........</h3>
<h4>...........</h4>
<h5>...........</h5>
<h6>...........</h6>
```

Attribute	Value	Description
1. align	left center right justify	Align attribute specifies the alignment of a heading.

Example for HTML heading tags.

```
<!DOCTYPE html>
<head>
<title> HTML headings example</title>
<body>
<h1 align="center">This is heading 1 Nirali Prakashan</h1>
<h2 align="left">This is heading 2 Nirali Prakashan </h2>
<h3>This is heading 3 Nirali Prakashan </h3>
<h4 align="right">This is heading 4 Nirali Prakashan </h4>
<h5 align="left">This is heading 5 Nirali Prakashan </h5>
<h6 align="center">This is heading 6 Nirali Prakashan </h6>
</body>
</head>
</html>
```

Output:

This is heading 1 Nirali Prakashan

This is heading 2 Nirali Prakashan

This is heading 3 Nirali Prakashan

This is heading 4 Nirali Prakashan

This is heading 5 Nirali Prakashan

This is heading 6 Nirali Prakashan

(iii) <p> Tag:

- HTML documents are divided into paragraphs.
- The HTML <p> tag is used for defining a paragraph.

  Syntax: `<p>...........</p>`

Attribute	Value	Description
1. align	left right center justify	Align attribute specifies the alignment of the text within a paragraph.

**(iv)
 Tag:**

- The HTML <br> tag is used for specifying a line break.
- The <br> tag is an empty tag. In other words, it has no end tag.

  Syntax: `<br/>`

Example for <p> and <br> tags.

```
<!DOCTYPE html>
<head>
<title> HTML paragraph example</title>
<body>
<p>A technical definition of the World Wide Web is all the resources and users on the Internet that are using the Hypertext Transfer Protocol (HTTP).
<br>W3C (World Wide Web Consortium), an international consortium of companies involved with the Internet and the Web.<br> HTML is a markup language. A markup language is a set of markup tags and the tags describes document content </p>
<p align="center">HTML stands for HyperText Markup Language.
</p>
<p>Hypertext <br> Text displayed on screen which can be accessed usually by a mouse click or key press. Apart from text, it can display other cool stuff like images, tables, frames etc.
</p>
<p align="left">Markup Language <br> Language which is used to structure data and present it to the user.
</p>
<p align="left">HTML is a language for describing web pages.</p>
</body>
</head>
</html>
```

Output:

A technical definition of the World Wide Web is all the resources and users on the Internet that are using the Hypertext Transfer Protocol (HTTP).
W3C (World Wide Web Consortium), an international consortium of companies involved with the Internet and the Web
HTML is a markup language. A markup language is a set of markup tags and the tags describes document content

HTML stands for Hyper Text Markup Language

Hypertext
Text displayed on screen which can be accessed usually by a mouse click or key press.
Apart from text, it can display other cool stuff like images, tables, frames etc.

Markup Language
Language which is used to structure data and present it to the user.

HTML is a language for describing web pages.

(v) <center> Tag:

- The <center> tag is used to center-align text.

(vi) Non breaking Spaces ( ):

- Suppose we were to use the phrase "14 Angry Men." Here we would not want a browser to split the "14" and "Angry" across two lines:
- A good example of this technique appears in the movie "14 Angry Men."
- In cases where we do not want the client browser to break text, we should use a nonbreaking space entity ( ) instead of a normal space.
- For example, when coding the "14 Angry Men" paragraph, we would use something similar to the following code:

```
<p>A good example of this technique appears in the movie "14 Angry Men."</p>
```

(vii) <div> Tag: [S-18, 17, W-17]

- The <div> tag defines a division or a section in an HTML document.
- The <div> tag is used to group block-elements to format them with CSS.

Syntax: `<div>............</div>`

Attribute	Value	Description
1. align	left right center justify	Align attribute specifies the alignment of the content inside a <div> element

Example for <div> tag.

```
<!DOCTYPE html>
<title> HTML div example</title>
<head></head>
<body>
<div style="background-color:orange;text-align:center">
<p>Nirali Prakashan</p>
</div>
```

```
<div style="background-color:pink;text-align:center">
<p>Pragati Group</p>
</div>
</body>
</html>
```

Output:

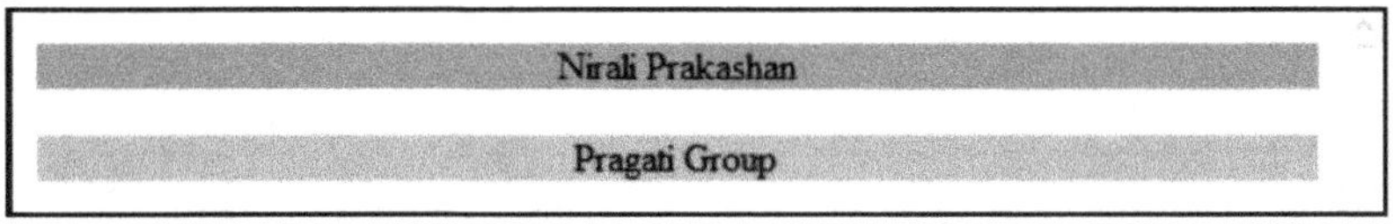

(viii) <span> Tag: [S-18, W-16, 17]

- The HTML <span> tag is used for grouping and applying styles to inline elements.
- The <span> tag provides a way to add a hook to a part of a text or a part of a document. The <span> tag provides no visual change by itself.
- The difference between the <span> tag and the <div> tag is that the <span> tag is used with inline elements while the <div> tag is used with block-level content.

  Syntax: `<span>..........</span>`

Example for <span> tag.

```
<!DOCTYPE html>
<head> span tag </head>
<title> HTML span tag example</title>
<body>
   <p>The <span style="color:red">span tag is used with inline elements</span> and the <span style="color:purple">div tag</span> is used with block-level content.</p>
</body>
</html>
```

Output:

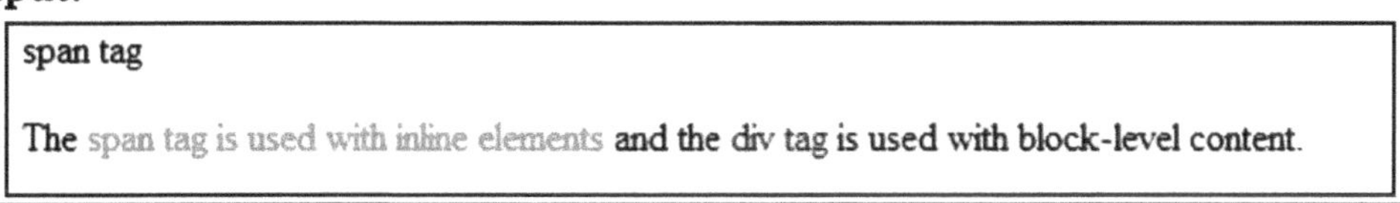

(ix) <hr> Tag:

- Horizontal rules are used to visually break up sections of a document. The HTML <hr> tag is used for specifying a horizontal rule in an HTML document.
- The <hr> tag creates a line from the current position in the document to the right margin and breaks the line accordingly.
- The <hr> tag is used to separate content (or define a change) in an HTML page.
- The intention behind the <hr> tag is that it indicates a paragraph-level break.

  Syntax: `<hr/>`

Attribute	Value	Description
1. align	left center right	This attribute specifies the alignment of a <hr> element.
2. noshade	noshade	This attribute specifies that a <hr> element should render in one solid color (noshaded), instead of a shaded color.
3. size	pixels	This attribute specifies the height of a <hr> element.
4. width	pixels %	This attribute specifies the width of a <hr> element.

Example for <hr> tag.

```
<!DOCTYPE html>
<head>
<title> HTML <hr> example</title>
</head>
<body>
<p>This is paragraph one and should be on top</p>
<hr align="right" width="50%">
<p>This is paragraph two and should be at middle</p>
<hr size="7">
<p>This is paragraph two and should be at bottom</p>
<hr width="80%" size="12" noshade>
</body>
</html>
```

Output:

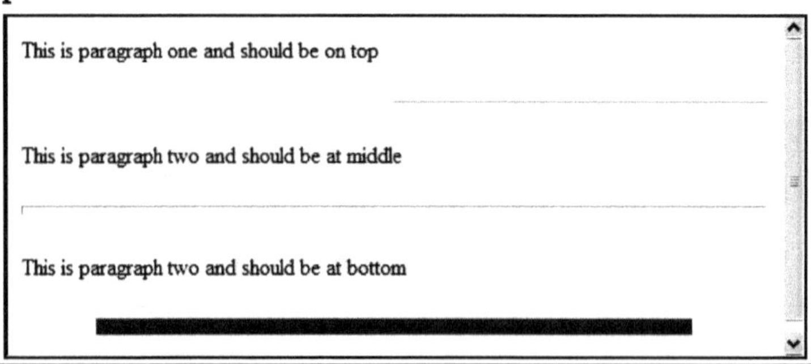

(x) HTML Marquees: **[S-19, 16]**

- A HTML marquee is a scrolling piece of text displayed either horizontally across or vertically down our web site page depending on the settings. This is created by using HTML tag <marquees>.

  Syntax:

```
<marquee attribute_name="attribute_value"....more attributes>
One or more lines or text message or image
</marquee>
```

- A HTML marquee can have following attributes:
  1. **width:** How wide the marquee is. This will have a value like 10 or 20%etc.
  2. **height:** How tall the marquee is. This will have a value like 10 or 20% etc.
  3. **direction:** Which direction the marquee should scroll. This will have value either up, down, left or right.
  4. **behaviour:** What type of scrolling. This will have value scroll, slide and alternate.
  5. **scrolldelay:** How long to delay between each jump. This will have a value like 10 etc.
  6. **scrollamount:** How far to jump. This will have a value like 10 etc.
  7. **loop:** How many times to loop. The default value is INFINITE, which means that the marquee loops endlessly.
  8. **bgcolor:** Background color. This will have any color name or color hex value.
  9. **hspace:** Horizontal space around the marquee. This will have a value like 10 or 20%etc.
  10. **vspace:** Vertical space around the marquee. This will have a value like 10 or 20%etc.

Example for HTML marques.

```
<!DOCTYPE html>
<head>
<title> HTML marquee tag</title>
</head>
<body>
<marquee>This is basic example of marquee tag in HTML</marquee>
<br/>
<br/>
<marquee width="50%">This example will take only 50% width</marquee>
<br/>
<br/>
<marquee direction="right">This text will scroll from left to
   right</marquee>
</body>
</html>
```

Output:

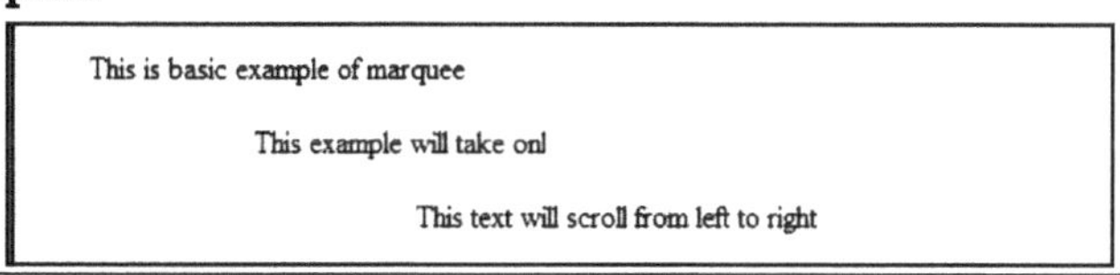

(xi) <font> Tag: **[W-16, S-17, 19]**

- <font> tag is used to add style, size, and color to the text on our site.
- The <font> tag specifies the font face, font size, and font color of text.

  Syntax: `<font>...........</font>`

Attribute	Value	Description
1. color	rgb(x,x,x) #xxxxxx colorname	This attribute specifies the color of text.
2. face	font_family	This attribute specifies the font of text.
3. size	number	This attribute specifies the size of text.

Example for <font> tag.

```
<!DOCTYPE html>
<head>
<title> HTML <font> example</title>
</head>
<body>
<p><h2>Nirali Prakashan</h2></p>
<font size="4" color="red">Wecome to Nirali Prakashan. <br/></font>
<font size="2" color="blue">Nirali Prakashan is a textbook publication firm.<br/></font>
<font face="verdana" color="black">Nirali Prakashan publised more than 3500 book titles.</font>
</body>
</html>
```

Output:

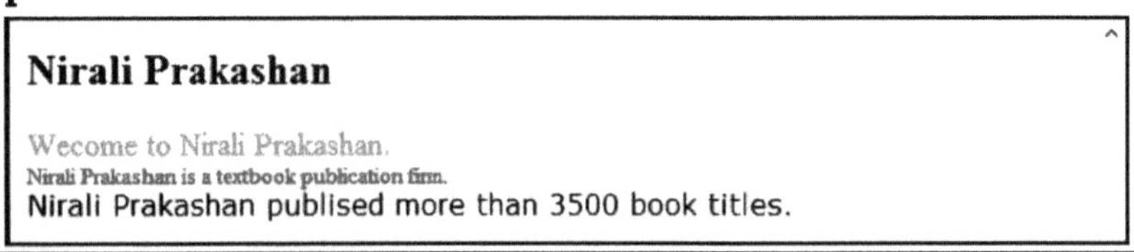

3.3.5 HTML Linking

- The real power of HTML is its ability to link to the other documents and pieces of text, images, video or audio.
- Links are usually highlighted or underlined in a document so that we know their existence. Clicking on the link opens up the document for viewing.
- Web pages can contain links that directly goes to other pages and even specific parts of a given page. These links are known as hyperlinks.
- Hyperlinks allow visitors to navigate between web sites by clicking on words, phrases, and images. Thus, we can create hyperlinks using text or images available on our any web page.
- A hyperlink (or link) is a word, group of words, or image that we can click on to jump to a new document or a new section within the current document.
- When we move the cursor over a link in a web page, the arrow will turn into a little hand.

1. <a> Anchor Tag: [S-17, W-17]

- The HTML <a> tag is used for creating a hyperlink to another web page.
- The <a> tag can be used in two ways:
  (i) To create a link to another document, by using the href attribute
  (ii) To create a bookmark inside a document, by using the name attribute
- The <a> tag defines a hyperlink, which is used to link from one page to another.
- By default, links will appear as follows in all browsers:
  - An unvisited link is underlined and blue.
  - A visited link is underlined and purple.
  - An active link is underlined and red.

Syntax: `<a href="Document URL">............</a>`

Attributes	Value	Description
1. charset	char_encoding	This attribute specifies the character-set of a linked document.
2. coords	coordinates	This attribute specifies the coordinates of a link.
3. href	URL	This attribute specifies the URL of the page the link goes to.
4. hreflang	language_code	This attribute specifies the language of the linked document.
5. media	media_query	This attribute specifies what media/device the linked document is optimized for.
6. name	section_name	This attribute specifies the name of an anchor.
7. rel	alternate author bookmark help license next nofollow noreferrer prefetch prev search tag	This attribute specifies the relationship between the current document and the linked document.
8. rev	text	This attribute specifies the relationship between the linked document and the current document.
9. shape	default rect circle poly	This attribute specifies the shape of a link.
10. target	_blank _parent _self _top framename	This attribute specifies where to open the linked document.
11. type	MIME_type	This attribute specifies the MIME type of the linked document.

Example for <a> tag.

```
<!DOCTYPE html>
<body>
<p>
<a href="default.asp">HTML</a> This is a link to a page on this website.
</p>
<p>
<a href="http://www.google.com/">Google</a> This is a link to a website on the World Wide Web.
</p>
</body>
</html>
```

Output:

> How to create hyperlinks
>
> HTML This is a link to a page on this website.
>
> Google This is a link to a website on the World Wide Web.

3.4 PHYSICAL AND LOGICAL HTML [W-17, S-16]

- The World Wide Web, like many hypertext systems, is based upon a markup language, in which authors annotate text to describe the texts role or appearance.
- There are two different views of markup, logical markup and physical markup. HTML has some logical tags and some physical tags.
- A tag that is applied to an individual character is known as a character tag. A character tag can be grouped into two categories i.e., physical and logical. (physical styles are associated with physical character tags; logical styles are associated with logical character tags.)
- The logical tags represent the structure and meaning of a document, with only suggested renderings for their appearance which may or may not be followed by various browsers under various system configurations.
- Following tables shows some common physical character tags.

Sr. No.	Tag	Description	Renders As
1.	`<b>`	bold	Displays text as bold.
2.	`<big>`	big	Displays text in a big font.
3.	`<i>`	italics	Displays text as italic.
4.	`<s>` or `<strike>`	strike	Displays text with a line through it.
5.	`<small>`	small	Displays text in a small font.

contd. ...

6.	<sub>	subscript	Displays the text as subscript — text that displays below the baseline of the text.
7.	<sup>	superscript	Displays the text as superscript — text that has baseline above the baseline of the rest of the text.
8.	<tt>	teletype	Displays the text with fixed-width font.
9.	<u>	underline	Underlines the text.

- The physical tags represent specific visual effects which are intended to be reproduced in a precise manner, and carry no connotation as to their semantic meaning.

3.5 HTML IMAGES [S-17, 18]

- Images are very important to beautify as well as to depicts many concepts on our web page.
- It is true that one single image is worth than thousands of words. So as a web developer we should have clear understanding on how to use images in our web pages.
- There are basically two types of graphic programs:
  1. Bitmap based.
  2. Vector based.
- The former comprises the image editing and painting programs while the latter refers to the drawing programs. Programs such as Adobe Photoshop, Corel Photo Paint and Painter, Macromedia Fireworks, etc. fall into the image editing and painting category.
- CorelDraw, Adobe Illustrator, and Macromedia Freehand are examples of vector-based drawing programs. Now many programs include tools for manipulating both types of images.
  1. **JPEG Images:** A JPEG file stands for Joint Photographic Experts Group. We would use a JPEG image for photographs, realistic scenes or other images with fine changes in tone.
  2. **GIF Images:** Images are limited to 256 colors; they are cross-platform, which means any computer can view them. GIF files are compressed, which makes them small in file size but not in dimension. GIF files unlike JPEG files do not lose quality in compression. GIF files have the .gif extension.
  3. **BMP:** Bitmap (BMP) is the standard Windows image format on DOS and Windows compatible computers. The BMP format supports RGB (red, green, blue) indexed-colors, grayscale, and Bitmap color modes. BMP files have the .bmp extension. A bitmap image is made up of pixels or bits (binary digits) of information arranged on a grid. Each bit can be visualized as a dot. The number of pixels per unit of measurement, example, ppi (pixels per inch) or dpi (dots per inch) determines the resolution of the image.

4. **PDF:** Portable Document Format (PDF) is used by Adobe Acrobat. PDF files can represent both vector and bitmap graphics and can contain electronic document search and navigation features such as electronic links. The PhotoShop PDF format supports RGB, indexed-colors, CMYK (cyan, magenta, yellow and black), grayscale and Bitmap. PhotoShop has the .pdf extension.
5. **TARGA:** TARGA is a raster graphics file format. This format is designed for systems using the true vision video board and is commonly supported by MS-DOS color applications. The Targa format supports 32 bit RGB, grayscale, and 16 bit and 24 bit RGB files without alpha channels. While saving an RGB image in this format, we can choose a pixel depth. Targa files have the .tga extension.
6. **TIFF:** Tagged-Image File Format (TIFF) is used to exchange files between applications and computer platforms. Virtually all paint programs, image editing, and page layout applications support TIFF format. Most of the older desktop scanners produce TIFF images and we should save images scanned as TIFF files unless we scan directly to PhotoShop. The TIFF format supports CMYK, RGB, and grayscale files. TIFF files have the .tif extension.
7. **PNG:** Portable Network Graphics (PNG) Pronounced "ping" was developed as an alternative to GIF. PNG files support 24-bit images and produces background transparency without pointed edges. Some older versions of web browsers may not support PNG images. Like GIF and JPEG files, PNG files are cross-platform and compressed. PNG files can have more colors than GIF files. PNG files have the .png extension.

1. **<img> Image Tag:**

- In HTML, images are defined with the <img> tag.
- The <img> tag is empty, which means that it contains attributes only, and has no closing tag.
- We will insert any image in our web page by using <img> tag.

Syntax: `<img src="image URL" attr_name="attr_value"... more attributes />`

Attributes	Value	Description
1. `alt`	`text`	This attribute specifies an alternate text for an image.
2. `src`	`URL`	This attribute specifies the URL of an image.

3. `align`	`top`
	`bottom`
	`middle`
	`left`
	`right`
		This attribute specifies the alignment of an image according to surrounding elements.

4. `alt`	`text`	This attribute specifies an alternate text for an image.
5. `border`	`pixels`	This attribute specifies the width of the border around an image.

contd. ...

6. crossoriginNew	anonymous use-credentials	This attribute allows images from third-party sites that allow cross-origin access to be used with canvas.
7. height	pixels	This attribute specifies the height of an image.
8. hspace	pixels	This attribute specifies the whitespace on left and right side of an image.
9. ismap	ismap	This attribute specifies an image as a server-side image-map.
10. longdesc	URL	This attribute specifies the URL to a document that contains a long description of an image.
11. src	URL	This attribute specifies the URL of an image.
12. usemap	#mapname	This attribute specifies an image as a client-side image-map.
13. vspace	pixels	This attribute specifies the whitespace on top and bottom of an image.
14. width	pixels	This attribute specifies the width of an image.

Example for image alignment: [TOP, MIDDLE, BOTTOM, LEFT, RIGHT].

```
<!DOCTYPE html>
<head>
<meta name="GENERATOR" content="MICROSOFT FRONTPAGE 4.0">
<meta name="PROGID" content="FRONTPAGE.EDITOR.DOCUMENT">
<title>IMAGE ALIGNMENT</title>
</head>
<body>
<center>THIS EXAMPLE IS FOR IMAGE ALIGNMENT:</center>
<p><img src = "smiley.gif" width="90" height="80" align ="top" border = 1>
HI, I AM SMILEY, A TOP TEXT</p>
<p><img src = "smiley.gif" width="90" height="80" align ="middle" border =
1> HI, I AM SMILEY, A MIDDLE TEXT</p>
<p><img src = "smiley.gif" width="90" height="80" align ="BOTTOM" border =
1> HI, I AM SMILEY, A BOTTOM TEXT</p>
<p><img src = "smiley.gif" width="90" height="80" align ="left" border = 1>
HI, I AM SMILEY, A TEXT AFTER IMAGE<br>YOU CAN WRITE A WHOLE PARAGRAPH<br>
ALSO AND CAN SEE IT AS <b>LEFT ALIGNMENT </b> </p><br>
<p><img src = "smiley.gif" width="90" height="80" align ="right" border =
1>HI, I AM SMILEY, A TEXT BEFORE IMAGE YOU CAN WRITE IN <b>RIGHT ALIGNMENT</b>
SAME THAT OF LEFT ALIGNMENT</p>
</body>
</html>
```

Output:

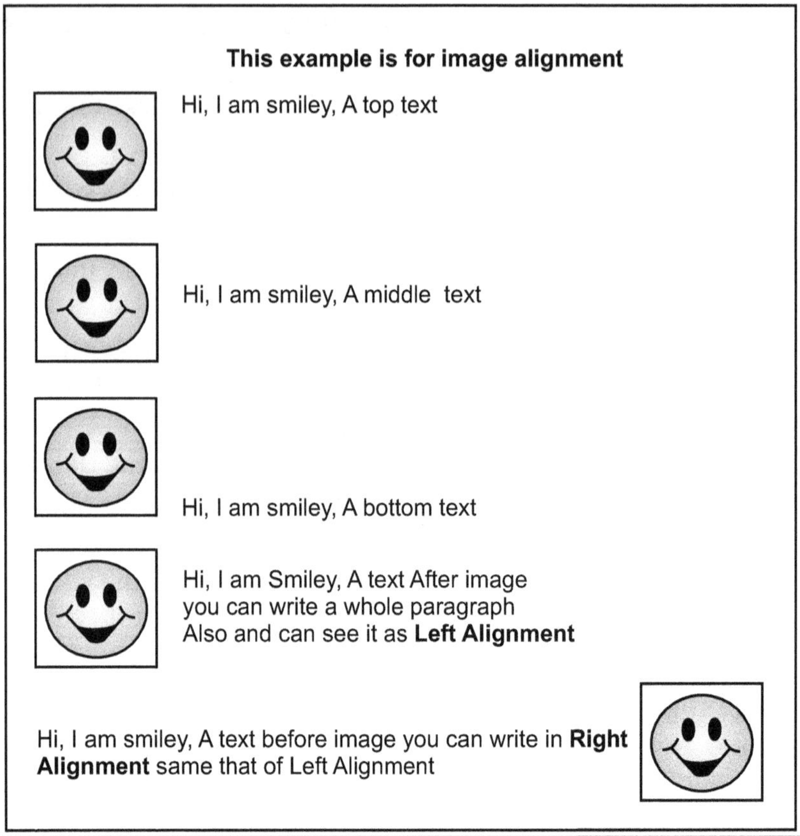

2. Image as a Link: [S-19, 17]

- Anything can be a link i.e. text or images. To make an image into a link we simply put the image tag inside the tag for a link.
- The tag would look like this:

```
<a href="http://www.anycartoonsite.com"><img src="z:\book\mikey.jpg"></a>
```

Example for image as link.

```
<!DOCTYPE html>
<body>
<p>Create a link of an image:
<a href="default.asp">
<img src="smiley.gif" alt="HTML tutorial" width="32" height="32" />
</a></p>
<p>No border around the image, but still a link:
<a href="default.asp">
<img border="0" src="smiley.gif" alt="HTML tutorial" width="32" height="32" />
</a></p>
</body>
</html>
```

Output:

Create a link of an image: 

No border around the image, but still a link: 

3. <area> Tag:

- The <area> tag defines an area inside an image-map (an image-map is an image with clickable areas).
- The <area> element is always nested inside a <map> tag.

Attribute	Value	Description
1. `alt`	`Text`	This attribute specifies an alternate text for an area.

3.5.1 Client-side and Server-side Image Mapping [W-16, 17]

- The is map attribute specifies that the image is part of a server-side image-map.
- The attributes ISMAP and USEMAP are basically used to give the server side and client side image maps.
- To use the client side image map, add the USEMAP attribute to the IMG element.

<map> Tag:

- The <map> tag is used to define a client-side image-map. An image-map is an image with clickable areas.
- The name attribute of the <map> element is required and it is associated with the <img> usemap attribute and creates a relationship between the image and the map.
- The <map> element contains a number of <area> elements, that defines the clickable areas in the image map.

1. Client-side Image Map:

Syntax: `<map>........</map>`

Attribute: `name=string`

- When we use a client-side image map, the information on the "hot spots" (clickable areas) in the image is defined here. Every selectable area should be mentioned in an area tag inside the <map> tag. The NAME attribute on the map tag assigns a name to the imagemap. The URL for the client-side image map should point to this.
- The ismap attribute specifies that the image is part of a server-side image-map.
- When clicking on a server-side image-map, the click coordinates are sent to the server as a URL query string.

Syntax: `<img ismap="ismap" />`

- For example, if we have a map named "foo", we could reference to it with:

`<img src="map.gif" usemap="#tst">` if the image was on the same page.

- Client-side image maps are not widely supported yet, so try to offer a textual alternative or also use a server-side image map. This can be done by putting the <img> tag with the use map attribute inside an A and by adding the ISMAP attribute.
- Having the image map data in a separate file is not as widely supported as inline data.

  There are two steps for creating client-side image maps:

  1. Define pixel location.
  2. Create a map file within the HTML document that contains our image map.
- For creating a client-side image map, we will need to specify our pixel locations as follows:

  RECTANGLE (RECT): Requires the upper left and lower right of the defined box.

  CIRCLE (CIRCLE): Requires the center point and radius (in pixels).

  POLYGON (POLYGON): Requires the co-ordinate of each vertex (point) of the area we want to define.

Example for client-side image map.

```
<!DOCTYPE html>
<head>
<meta name="GENERATOR" content="MICROSOFT FRONTPAGE 4.0">
<meta name="PROGID" content="FRONTPAGE.EDITOR.DOCUMENT">
<title> client side Image Map 1</title>
</head>
<body>
<img src="SAMPLE.GIF" usemap="#TEST">
<map name="TEST">
   <area shape="RECT" coords="26,72,145,146" href="RECT.HTML">
   <area shape="CIRCLE" coords="262,110,42" href="CIRCLE.HTML">
   <area shape="POLYGON" coords="389,64,440,64,465,105,440,
   147,389,147,365,105" href ="POLY.HTML">
<area shape="RECT" coords="0,0,499,212" href="BASERECT.HTML">
</map>
</body>
</html>
```

Output:

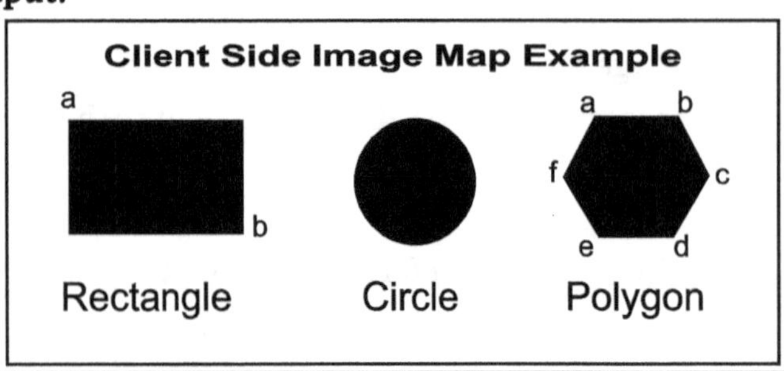

- Now in the above document we can see that the image map is created and the program is enclosing all the co-ordinates of each and every point.
- When we will click the Blue rectangle then it will take us to the rect.html file.
- When we will click the Red circle then it will take us to the circle.html file. And so on.
- If we are unable to create the proper map file nothing will happen if we click a shape.

2. Server Side Image Map:

- The usemap attribute specifies an image as a client-side image-map.
- An image-map is an image with clickable areas.
- The usemap attribute is associated with a <map> element's name or id attribute, and creates a relationship between the image and the map.

  Syntax: `<img usemap="#mapname" />`

  Attribute values:

  1. `#mapname`: A hash character ("#") plus the name or id of the map element to use
- There are three steps for creating a server side image map:
  1. Define our pixel locations.
  2. Create an external map file.
  3. Insert a special address into the HTML document that contains our server side image map.

Step 1:

- For creating a client side image map, we will need to specify our pixel locations as follows:
  - **RECTANGLE (RECT):** Requires the upper left and lower right of the defined box.
  - **CIRCLE (CIRCLE):** Requires the center point and radius (in pixels).
  - **POLYGON (POLYGON):** Requires the co-ordinate of EACH vertex (point) of the area we want to define.

Step 2:

- Create a text (ASCII) file and save it with the extension .map. Put this file in the same directory as our HTML document that references our GIF image. In the file, we should include: A default URL. This is a location that a person will go to if she/he clicks on a part of our image map that is not a hot spot. We must specify a default URL for our server side image map to work. In the map file that follows, the default URL is line 1. our tags (i.e., default, rect, circle, and poly) must be in lowercase.

Step 3:

- Insert a special address into the HTML document that contains our server side image map. This address should include:
  1. The anchored hyperlink reference (A HREF) that specifies the location of the external map file and server side image map program on the NCSA web server. In the address that follows, this reference is line 1. We will need to replace the bold text with our server and the path to our map file, respectively.
  2. The GIF used for our image map. In the address that follows:

```
<a href="server.map">
<img src="server.gif" ismap>
```

3.6 LIST, TABLE, FRAMES

3.6.1 List [S-16, W-17]

- We can list out our items, subjects or menu in the form of a list. HTML gives us three different types of lists, i.e. an unordered list (This will list items using bullets), a ordered list (This will use different schemes of numbers to list our items) and a definition list (This is arrange our items in the same way as they are arranged in a dictionary).

1. Unordered Lists: [S-19, 16, W-16]

- An unordered list is a collection of related items that have no special order or sequence.
- The most common unordered list, we will find on the web is a collection of hyperlinks to other documents.
- Unordered list is created by using <ul> tag. Each item in the list is marked with a bullet. The bullet itself comes in three types: squares, discs, and circles. The default bullet displayed by most web browsers is the traditional full disc.

Syntax: `<ul>.........</ul>`

Attributes	Value	Description
1. compact	compact	This attribute specifies that the list should render smaller than normal.
2. type	disc square circle	This attribute specifies the kind of marker to use in the list.

Example for <ul> tag.

```
<!DOCTYPE html>
<body>
<head><h3>An Unordered List Example</h3>
<h4>Disc bullets list:</h4>
<ul type="disc">
    <li>Apples</li>
    <li>Bananas</li>
    <li>Lemons</li>
    <li>Oranges</li>
</ul>
<h4>Circle bullets list:</h4>
<ul type="circle">
    <li>Apples</li>
    <li>Bananas</li>
    <li>Lemons</li>
```

```
    <li>Oranges</li>
</ul>
<h4>Square bullets list:</h4>
<ul type="square">
    <li>Apples</li>
    <li>Bananas</li>
    <li>Lemons</li>
    <li>Oranges</li>
</ul>
</body>
</head>
</html>
```

Output:

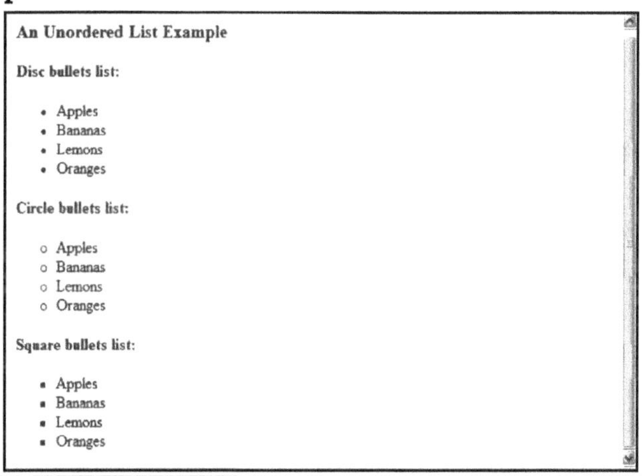

- We can also nested unordered list as follows:

```
<!DOCTYPE html>
<body>
<h4>A nested List:</h4>
<ul>
    <li>Coffee</li>
    <li>Tea
    <ul>
    <li>Black tea</li>
    <li>Green tea
    <ul>
    <li>China</li>
    <li>Africa</li>
```

```
        </ul>
        </li>
        </ul>
        </li>
        <li>Milk</li>
    </ul>
    </body>
    </html>
```

Output:

A nested List:

- Coffee
- Tea
    - Black tea
    - Green tea
        - China
        - Africa
- Milk

2. Ordered Lists: **[S-19, 16, W-16]**

- The typical browser formats the contents of an ordered list just like an unordered list, except that the items are numbered instead of bulleted.
- The numbering starts at one and is incremented by one for each successive ordered list element tagged with <li> tag.
- Ordered list is created by using <ol> tag. Each item in the list is marked with a number.

Syntax: `<ol>............</ol>`

Attributes	Value	Description
1. compact	compact	This attribute specifies that the list should render smaller than normal.
2. reversed	reversed	This attribute specifies that the list order should be descending like 9,8,7...
3. start	number	This attribute specifies the start value of an ordered list.
4. type	1 A a I i	This attribute specifies the kind of marker to use in the list.

Example for <ol> tag.

```
<!DOCTYPE html>
<head>
<body>
<head><h3>An Ordered List Example</h3>
<h4>Numbered list:</h4>
<ol>
   <li>Apples</li>
    <li>Bananas</li>
   <li>Lemons</li>
</ol>
<h4>Letters list:</h4>
<ol type="A">
   <li>Apples</li>
   <li>Bananas</li>
   <li>Lemons</li>
</ol>
<h4>Lowercase letters list:</h4>
<ol type="a">
   <li>Apples</li>
   <li>Bananas</li>
   <li>Lemons</li>
</ol>
<h4>Roman numbers list:</h4>
<ol type="I">
   <li>Apples</li>
   <li>Bananas</li>
   <li>Lemons</li>
</ol>
<h4>Lowercase Roman numbers list:</h4>
<ol type="i">
   <li>Apples</li>
   <li>Bananas</li>
   <li>Lemons</li>
</ol>
</body>
</head>
</html>
```

Output:

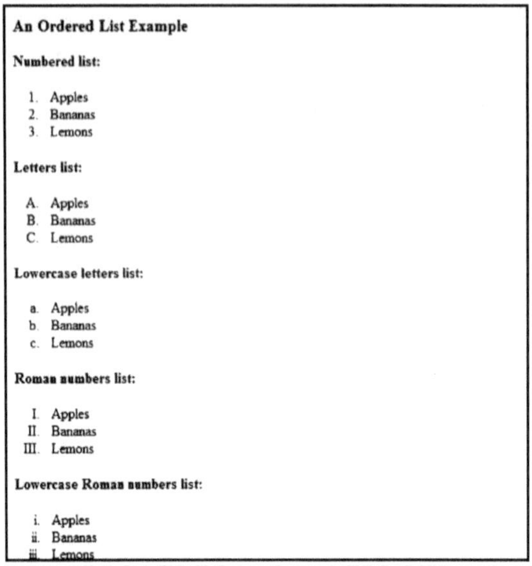

An Ordered List Example

Numbered list:

1. Apples
2. Bananas
3. Lemons

Letters list:

A. Apples
B. Bananas
C. Lemons

Lowercase letters list:

a. Apples
b. Bananas
c. Lemons

Roman numbers list:

I. Apples
II. Bananas
III. Lemons

Lowercase Roman numbers list:

i. Apples
ii. Bananas
iii. Lemons

3. Definition Lists:

- HTML and XHTML also support a list style entirely different from the ordered and unordered lists we have discussed i.e. definition lists.
- Like the entries we find in a dictionary or encyclopedia, complete with text, pictures, and other multimedia elements, the Definition List is the ideal way to present a glossary, list of terms, or other name/value list.
- Definition List makes use of following three tags.
  - <dl> - Defines the start of the list.
  - <dt> - A term.
  - <dd> - Term definition.
  - </dl> - Defines the end of the list.
- A definition list is a list of items, with a description of each item.
- The definition list is the ideal way to present a glossary, list of terms, or other name/value list.

  Syntax: `<dl>............</dl>`
- Definition List makes use of following two tags.

  (i) <dt>: The dt tag is used inside dl. It marks up a term whose definition is provided by the next dd. The dt tag may only contain text-level markup.

  (ii) <dd>: The <dd> tag is used inside a dl definition list to provide the definition of the text in the dt tag. It may contain block elements but also plain text and markup.

Example for definition list.

```
<!DOCTYPE html>
<body>
<h4>A Definition List:</h4>
```

```
<dl>
   <dt>Coffee</dt>
   <dd>Black hot drink</dd>
   <dt>Milk</dt>
   <dd>White cold drink</dd>
</dl>
</body>
</html>
```

Output:

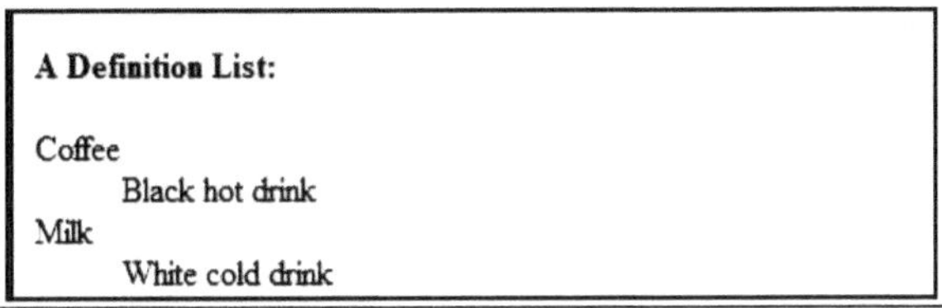

<meta> Tag:

- Meta elements are typically used to specify page description, keywords, author of the document, last modified, and other metadata. The <meta> tag always goes inside the head element. Metadata is data (information) about data.
- The HTML <meta> tag is used for declaring metadata for the HTML document. Metadata will not be displayed on the page, but will be machine parsable.

  Syntax: `<meta name = string content = string>`
- Metadata can include document description, keywords, author etc. It can also be used to refresh the page or set cookies.
- The <meta> tag is placed between the opening/closing <head> tags.

Example for <meta> tag.

```
<!DOCTYPE html>
<head>
<title>Meta Refresh Example</title>
<meta http-equiv="refresh"
content="5;url=/html_5/tags/html_meta_tag_example.cfm" />
</head>
<body style="background-color:#ff9900;">
<p>Watch me redirect to another page in 5 seconds...</p>
</body>
</html>
```

Output:

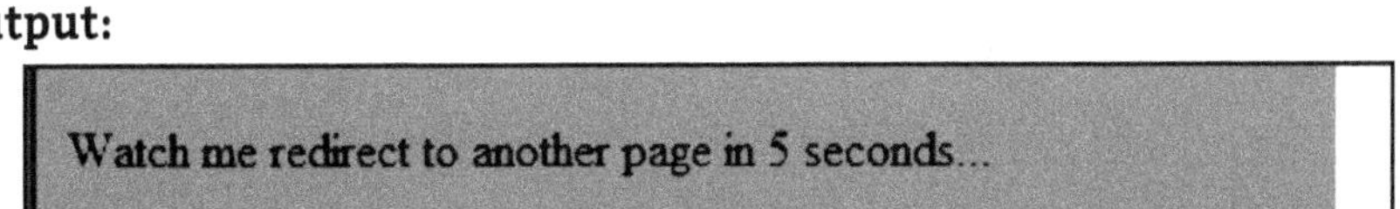

<li>List Tag:

- The <li> tag defines a list item.
- The <li> tag is used in ordered lists (<ol>), unordered lists (<ul>), and in menu lists (<menu>).

Syntax: `<li>.........</li>`

Attributes	Value	Description
1. type	1 A a I i disc square circle	This attribute specifies which kind of bullet point will be used.
2. value	number	This attribute specifies the value of a list item.

3.6.2 Tables [S-19]

- Tables are very useful to arrange in HTML and they are used very frequently by almost all web developers.
- Tables are just like spreadsheets and they are made up of rows and columns.
- The HTML table model allows to arrange data - text, preformatted text, images, links, forms, form fields, other tables etc. into rows and columns of cells.
- Using tables to divide the page into different sections is an extremely powerful tool.

1. <table> Tag:

- The <table> tag defines an HTML table.
- An HTML table consists of the <table> element and one or more <tr>, <th>, and <td> elements. The <tr> element defines a table row, the <th> element defines a table header, and the <td> element defines a table cell.

Syntax: `<table>............</table>`

Attributes	Value	Description
1. align	left center right	This attribute specifies the alignment of a table according to surrounding text.
2. bgcolor	rgb(x,x,x) #xxxxxx colorname	This attribute specifies the background color for a table.
3. border	pixels	This attribute specifies the width of the borders around a table.
4. cellpadding	pixels	This attribute specifies the space between the cell wall and the cell content.

contd. ...

5. cellspacing	pixels	This attribute specifies the space between cells.
6. frame	void above below hsides lhs rhs vsides box border	This attribute specifies which parts of the outside borders that should be visible.
7. rules	none groups rows cols all	This attribute specifies which parts of the inside borders that should be visible.
8. summary	text	This attribute specifies a summary of the content of a table.
9. width	pixels %	This attribute specifies the width of a table.

2. <th> Tag:

- Table heading can be defined using <th> tag or the <th> tag defines a header cell in an HTML table. This tag will be put to replace <td> tag which is used to represent actual data.
- An HTML table has two kinds of cells:
  - **Header cells:** contains header information (created with the <th> element), and
  - **Standard cells:** contains data (created with the <td> element).
- The text in <th> elements are bold and centered by default.

  Syntax: `<th>...........</th>`

3. <tr> Tag:

- The <tr> tag defines a row in an HTML table.
- A <tr> element contains one or more <th> or <td> elements.

  Syntax: `<tr>...........<tr>`

4. <td> Tag:

- The <td> tag defines a standard cell in an HTML table.
- The <td> tag is used to mark up individual cells inside a table row.
- The text in <td> elements are regular and left-aligned by default.

  Syntax: `<td>...........</td>`

Example for <table>, <th>, <tr> and <td>tag.

```
<!DOCTYPE html>
<head>
<body>
<table border="1">
<tr>
<th>Name</th>
<th>Salary</th>
</tr>
<tr>
<td>Ramesh Salunkhe</td>
<td>50,000</td>
</tr>
<tr>
<td>Amar Salvi</td>
<td>75,000</td>
</tr>
</table>
</body>
</head>
</html>
```

Output:

Name	Salary
Ramesh Salunkhe	50,000
Amar Salvi	75,000

5. <caption> Tag:

- The <caption> tag defines a table caption.
- The <caption> tag is used to provide a caption for a table. This caption can either appear above or below the table. This can be indicated with the align attribute.

  Syntax: <caption>............<caption>
- The <caption> tag must be inserted immediately after the <table> tag.
- We can specify only one caption per table.

Attribute	Value	Description
1. align	left right top bottom	This attribute defines the alignment of a caption.

Example for <caption> tag.

```
<!DOCTYPE html>
<body>
<table border="1">
   <caption>Monthly Savings</caption>
<tr>
   <th>Month</th>
   <th>Savings</th>
</tr>
<tr>
   <td>January</td>
   <td>Rs. 1000</td>
</tr>
<tr>
   <td>February</td>
   <td> Rs. 1500</td>
</tr>
</table>
</body>
</html>
```

Output:

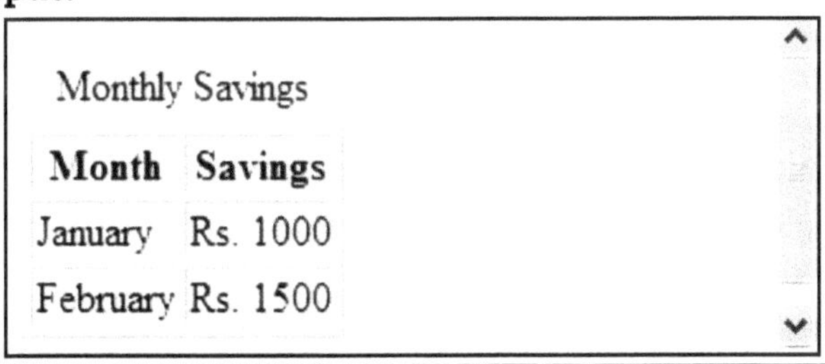

Monthly Savings

Month	Savings
January	Rs. 1000
February	Rs. 1500

6. Cellpadding and Cellspacing in a Table:

- There are two attribiutes called cellpadding and cellspacing which we will use to adjust the white space in our table cell.
- Cellspacing defines the width of the border, while cellpadding represents the distance between cell borders and the content within it.

Example for cellspacing.

```
<!DOCTYPE html>
<body>
<h4>Without  cellspacing:</h4>
<table border="1">
<tr>
   <td>First</td>
```

```
    <td>Row</td>
  </tr>
  <tr>
    <td>Second</td>
    <td>Row</td>
  </tr>
  </table>
  <h4>With cellspacing="0":</h4>
  <table border="1" cellspacing="0">
  <tr>
    <td>First</td>
    <td>Row</td>
  </tr>
  <tr>
    <td>Second</td>
    <td>Row</td>
  </tr>
  </table>
  <h4>With cellspacing="10":</h4>
  <table border="1" cellspacing="10">
  <tr>
    <td>First</td>
    <td>Row</td>
  </tr>
  <tr>
    <td>Second</td>
    <td>Row</td>
  </tr>
  </table>
  </body>
  </html>
```

Output:

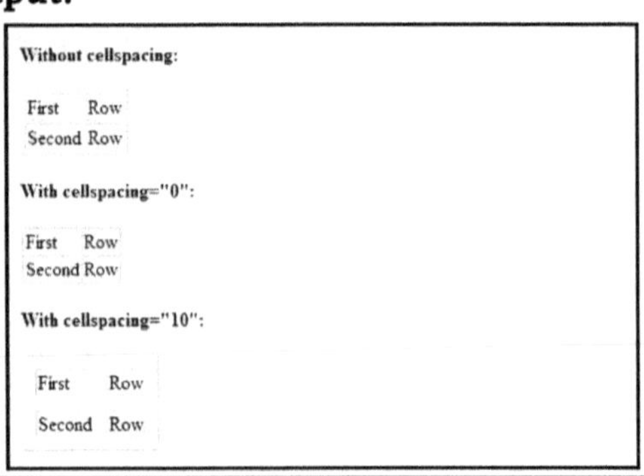

Example for cellpadding.

```
<!DOCTYPE html>
<body>
<h4>Without cellpadding:</h4>
<table border="1">
<tr>
   <td>First</td>
    <td>Row</td>
</tr>
<tr>
   <td>Second</td>
   <td>Row</td>
</tr>
</table>
<h4>With cellpadding:</h4>
<table border="1"
cellpadding="10">
<tr>
   <td>First</td>
   <td>Row</td>
</tr>
<tr>
   <td>Second</td>
   <td>Row</td>
</tr>
</table>
</body>
</html>
```

Output:

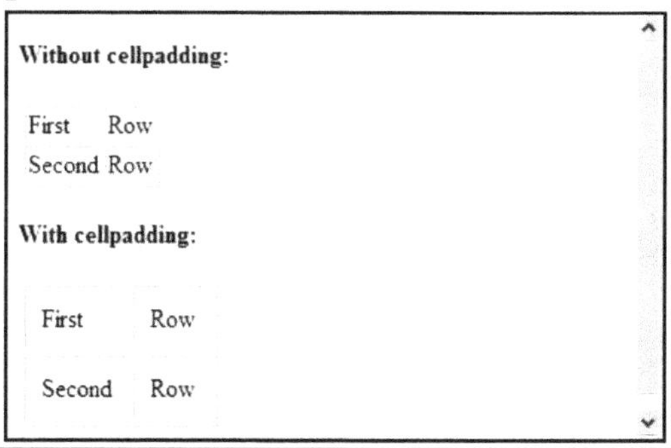

7. Colspan and Rowspan attributes in Table:

- We will use colspan attribute if we want to merge two or more columns into a single column. Similar way we will use rowspan if we want to merge two or more rows.

Example for colspan and rowspan.

```
<!DOCTYPE html>
<head>
<title>Practice HTML table spans</title>
</head>
<body>
<p>Merge two or more rows or columns and then see the result:</p>
<table border="1">
<tr>
<th>Column 1</th>
<th>Column 2</th>
<th>Column 3</th>
</tr>
<tr><td rowspan="2">Row 1 Cell 1</td>
<td>Row 1 Cell 2</td><td>Row 1 Cell 3</td></tr>
<tr><td>Row 2 Cell 2</td><td>Row 2 Cell 3</td></tr>
<tr><td colspan="3">Row 3 Cell 1</td></tr>
</table>
</body>
</html>
```

Output:

Merge two or more rows or columns and then see the result:

<table border="1">
<tr><th>Column 1</th><th>Column 2</th><th>Column 3</th></tr>
<tr><td rowspan="2">Row 1 Cell 1</td><td>Row 1 Cell 2</td><td>Row 1 Cell 3</td></tr>
<tr><td>Row 2 Cell 2</td><td>Row 2 Cell 3</td></tr>
<tr><td colspan="3">Row 3 Cell 1</td></tr>
</table>

8. Table Backgrounds:

- We can set table background using the following two ways:
    1. **Using bgcolor attribute:** We can set background color for whole table or just for one cell.
    2. **Using background attribute:** We can set background image for whole table or just for one cell.

Example for setting tables background.

```
<!DOCTYPE html>
<head>
<title>Practice HTML table background colors</title>
</head>
<body>
<table border="1">
<tr title="You are looking at Row 1" bgcolor="silver">
    <td>Row 1 Cell 1</td>
    <td>Row 1 Cell 2</td>
</tr>
<tr title="You are looking at Row 2" bgcolor="aqua">
    <td>Row 2 Cell 1</td>
    <td>Row 2 Cell 2</td>
</tr>
</table>
</body>
</html>
```

Output:

Row 1 Cell 1	Row 1 Cell 2
Row 2 Cell 1	Row 2 Cell 2

Example: Write HTML code to design the following output:

Population Table

Country	Population (in crores)	
India	2000 2004 2008	100 105 110
USA	2000 2004 2008	40 45 50

Sol.:

```
<html>
    <head>
        <title>Population Table</title>
    </head>
    <body>
```

```
        <table border=1>
            <caption>Population Table</caption>
            <tr>
                <th>Country</th>
                <th colspan="2">Population (in crores)</th>
            </tr>
            <tr>
                <td rowspan="3">India</td>
                <td>2000</td>
                <td>100</td>
            </tr>
            <tr>
                <td>2004</td>
                <td>105</td>
            </tr>
            <tr>
                <td>2008</td>
                <td>110</td>
            </tr>
            <tr>
                <td rowspan="3">USA</td>
                <td>2000</td>
                <td>40</td>
            </tr>
            <tr>
                <td>2004</td>
                <td>45</td>
            </tr>
            <tr>
                <td>2008</td>
                <td>50</td>
            </tr>
        </table>
</body>
</html>
```

Example: Write html code to design following output frame: **[S-17, W-16]**

<table>
<tr><th colspan="2">BCA</th></tr>
<tr><td>TYBCA</td><td><ul><li>Java</li><li>Web Tech</li><li>OOPS</li><li>Dot Net</li></ul></td></tr>
</table>

Sol.:

```
<html>
    <head>
        <title>FRAME</title>
    </head>
    <body>
        <table border=1>
        <tr>
            <th colspan="2">BCA</th>
        </tr>
        <tr>
            <td>TYBCA</td>
            <td>
                <ul>
                    <li>Java</li>
                    <li>Web Tech</li>
                    <li>OOPS</li>
                    <li>Dot Net</li>
                </ul>
            </td>
        </tr>
    </table>
</body>
</html>
```

Example: Write HTML code to design the following output for table: **[S-18, 19, W-17, 16]**

Train Time-Table			
TNO	**TName**	**Arrival Time**	**Departure Time**
T0001	Mumbai Express	2:00 PM	2:30 PM

Sol.:

```
<html>
<body>
<table border=1 align="center">
<tr align="center">
<td colspan=4><h1>Train Time-Table</h1></td>
</tr>
<tr align="center">
<td>TNO</td>
<td>TNAME</td>
```

```
<td>Arrival Time</td>
<td>Departure Time</td>
</tr>
<tr align="center">
<td>T0001</td>
<td>Mumbai Express</td>
<td>2:00 PM</td>
<td>2:30 PM</td>
</tr>
</table>
</body>
</html>
```

Example: Write HTML code to design following output for table: **[S-17]**

Supplier Name	Product Name	Product Details		Total Price
		Price	Quantity	
Poonam Electronics	Printers	2500	08	20000
Raj Electronics	Scanner	1800	05	9000

Sol.:

```
<html>
<title>prr3</title>
<body><center>
<table border="2" cellpadding="12">
<tr>
<th rowspan=2><center>Supplier Name</center></th>
<th rowspan=2><center>Product Name</center></th>
<th colspan="2"><center>Product Details</center></th>
<th rowspan=2><center>Total Price</center></th>
</tr>
<tr>
<td><center>Price</center></td>
<td><center>Quantity</center></td>
</tr>
<tr>
<td>Poonam Electronics</td>
<td>Printers</td>
<td>2500</td>
```

```
<td>08</td>
<td>20000</td>
</tr>
<tr>
<td>Raj Electronics</td>
<td>Scanner </td>
<td>1800</td>
<td>05</td>
<td>9000</td>
</tr>
</table>
</body>
</html>
```

3.6.3 Frames [W-16, 17, S-18]

- The term frames is used as shorthand for "a technique to display multiple documents at once". This technique is only used when the browser is running on a graphical display.
- Frames allow us to split the browser window into multiple windows that can display different pages. This will make the navigation much easier for the visitor.
- With frames, we can display more than one HTML document in the same browser window. Each HTML document is called a frame, and each frame is independent of the others.
- Frames divide a browser window into several pieces or panes, each pane containing a separate XHTML/HTML document.
- One of the key advantages that frames offer is that we can then load and reload single panes without having to reload the entire contents of the browser window.
- A collection of frames in the browser window is known as a frameset.
- The window is divided up into frames in a similar pattern to the way tables are organized: into rows and columns. The simplest framesets might just divide the screen into two rows, while a complex frameset could use several rows and columns.
- Frames are used to display more than one document in the same window.
- Frames are defined in <frameset>, and inside it we have <frame> which defines the location of the web page to load into the frame. See the example given below to understand it clearly.

Example for vertical frames.

```
<!DOCTYPE html>
<frameset cols="50%,30%,20%">
<frame src="frame1.html" />
<frame src="frame2.html" />
<frame src="frame3.html" />
</frameset>
</html>
```

Output:

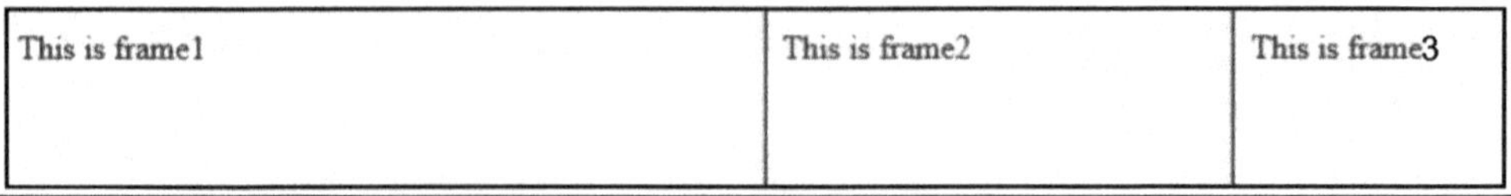

Example for horizontal frames.

```
<!DOCTYPE html>
<frameset rows="50%,30%,20%">
<frame src="frame1.html" />
<frame src="frame2.html" />
<frame src="frame3.html" />
</frameset>
</html>
```

Output:

1. <frame> Tag:

- The <frame> tag indicates what goes in each frame of the frameset.
- The <frame> element is always an empty element, and therefore should not have any content, although each <frame> element should always carry one attribute, src, to indicate the page that should represent that frame.
- The <frame> tag defines one particular window (frame) within a <frameset> and each <frame> in a <frameset> can have different attributes, such as border, scrolling, the ability to resize, etc.

Syntax: `<frame>………</frame>`

Attributes	Value	Description
1. frameborder	0 1	This attribute specifies whether or not to display a border around a frame.
2. longdesc	URL	This attribute specifies a page that contains a long description of the content of a frame.
3. marginheight	pixels	This attribute specifies the top and bottom margins of a frame.
4. marginwidth	pixels	This attribute specifies the left and right margins of a frame.
5. name	name	This attribute specifies the name of a frame.

contd. …

6. noresize	noresize	This attribute specifies that a frame cannot be resized.
7. scrolling	yes no auto	This attribute specifies whether or not to display scrollbars in a frame.
8. src	URL	This attribute specifies the URL of the document to show in a frame.

2. <frameset> tag: **[S-17, 19]**

- The <frameset> tag holds one or more frame elements. Each frame element can hold a separate document.
  - The <frameset> tag replaces the <body> element in frameset documents.
  - The <frameset> tag defines how to divide the window into frames.
  - Each frameset defines a set of rows or columns. If we define frames by using rows then horizontal frames are created. If we define frames by using columns then vertical frames are created.
  - The values of the rows/columns indicate the amount of screen area each row/column will occupy.
  - Each frame is indicated by <frame> tag and it defines what HTML document to put into the frame.
- Following are important attributes of <frameset> and should be known to us to use frameset.

  (i) cols: specifies how many columns are contained in the frameset and the size of each column. We can specify the width of each column in one of four ways:
  - Absolute values in pixels. For example to create three vertical frames, use cols="100, 500,100".
  - A percentage of the browser window. For example to create three vertical frames, use cols="10%, 80%,10%".
  - Using a wildcard symbol. For example to create three vertical frames, use cols="10%, *,10%". In this case wildcard takes remainder of the window.
  - As relative widths of the browser window. For example to create three vertical frames, use cols="3*,2*,1*". This is an alternative to percentages. We can use relative widths of the browser window. Here the window is divided into sixths: the first column takes up half of the window, the second takes one third, and the third takes one sixth.

  (ii) rows: attribute works just like the cols attribute and can take the same values, but it is used to specify the rows in the frameset. For example to create two horizontal frames, use rows="10%, 90%". We can specify the height of each row in the same way as explained above for columns.

  (iii) border: attribute specifies the width of the border of each frame in pixels. For example border="5". A value of zero specifies that no border should be there.

(iv) frameborder: specifies whether a three-dimensional border should be displayed between frames. This attribute takes value either 1 (yes) or 0 (no). For example frameborder="0" specifies no border.

(v) framespacing: specifies the amount of space between frames in a frameset. This can take any integer value. For example framespacing="10" means there should be 10 pixels spacing between each frames.

Example for frameset element defining rows and columns.

```
<!DOCTYPE html>
<head>
<meta name="GENERATOR" content="Microsoft FrontPage 4.0">
<meta name="ProgId" content="FrontPage.Editor.Document">
<title>Frameset Element Defining Rows and Columns</title>
</head>
<frameset rows="64,*,64">
<frame src="z:\comp.html">
<frameset cols="150,*">
<frame src="z:\about.html">
<frame src="z:\dept1.html">
</frameset>
<frame src="z:\it.html">
</frameset>
</html>
```

Output:

3. <noframes> Tag:

- If a user is using any old browser or any browser which does not support frames then <noframes> element should be displayed to the user.

  Syntax: `<noframes>............</noframes>`

- The noframes element contains content that should only be rendered when frames are not displayed. noframes is typically used in a frameset document to provide alternate content for browsers that do not support frames or have frames disabled.

Example for <noframes> tag.

```
<!DOCTYPE html>
<head>
<meta name="generator" content="Microsoft FrontPage 4.0">
<meta name="ProgId" content="FrontPage.Editor.Document">
<title>a frameset document which has a noframes alternative</title>
</head>
<frameset rows="*,*">
<frame src="z:\comp.html" name=foo>
<frame src="z:\etc.html" name=bar>
<noframes>
<body>
this is the noframes alternative section.
any block-level html element may be used here.
</body>
</noframes>
</frameset>
</html>
```

Output:

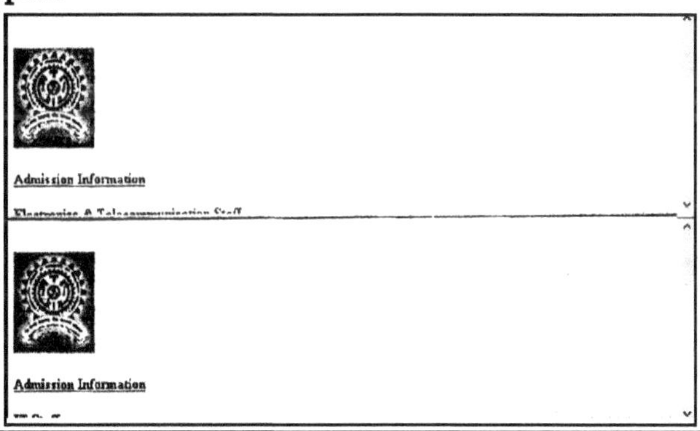

4. <iframe> Tag:

- We can define an inline frame with the <iframe> tag.
- The <iframe> tag is not used within a <frameset> tag. Instead, it appears anywhere in our document.
- The <iframe> tag defines a rectangular region within the document in which the browser displays a separate document, including scrollbars and borders.
- Use the src attribute with <iframe> to specify the URL of the document that occupies the inline frame.
- All of the other, optional attributes for the <iframe> tag, including name, class, frameborder, id, longdesc, marginheight, marginwidth, name, scrolling, style, and title behave exactly like the corresponding attributes for the <frame> tag.

Example for <iframe> tag.

```
<html>
<head>
<title>IFrames example</title>
</head>
<body>
<p>...other document content...</p>
<iframe src="/html/menu.htm" width="100" height="200" align="right">
Your browser does not support inline frames. To view this
<a href="/html/menu.htm">Menu</a> correctly, you'll need
a copy of Internet Explorer or the latest Netscape Navigator.
</iframe>
<p>...subsequent document content...</p>
</body>
</html>
```

5. Frame's name and target attributes:

- One of the most popular uses of frames is to place navigation bars in one frame and then load the pages with the content into a separate frame.

```
<!DOCTYPE html>
<head>
<title>Frames example</title>
</head>
<frameset cols="200, *">
   <frame src="/html/menu.htm" name="menu_page" />
   <frame src="/html/main.htm" name="main_page" />
   <noframes>
   <body>
   Your browser does not support frames.
   </body>
   </noframes>
</frameset>
</html>
```

Write HTML Code to create the following frame.

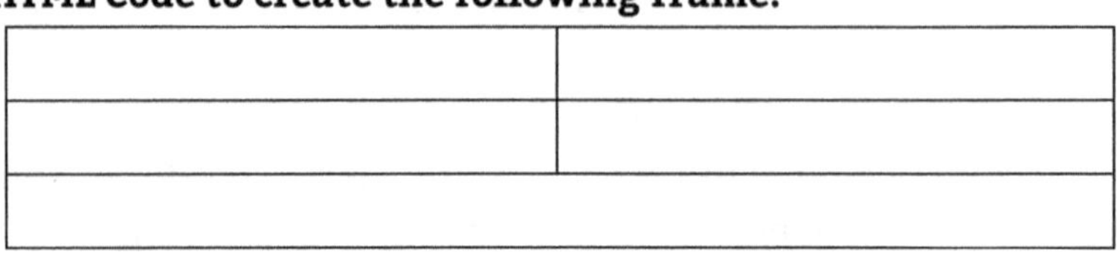

Sol.:

```
<html>
<frameset rows="66%,*">
<frameset cols="50%,50%">
   <frameset rows="50%,50%">
      <frame>
      <frame>
</frameset>
   <frameset rows="50%,50%">
      <frame>
      <frame>
   </frameset>
</frameset>
<frame>
</frameset>
</html>
```

Write HTML code to display the following frame. **[W-17]**

<table>
<tr><td colspan="3">One</td></tr>
<tr><td colspan="2">two</td><td>three</td></tr>
<tr><td>four</td><td>five</td><td>six</td></tr>
</table>

Sol.:

```
<html>
<frameset rows="30%,*">
<frame name="one">
<frameset rows="50%,50%" cols="50%,50%">
<frame name="topleft">
<frame name="topright">
<frameset cols="70%,30%">
<frame name="brtl">
<frame name="brtr">
</frameset>
<frame name="botrbot">
</frameset>
</frameset>
</html>
```

3.7 EMBEDDING AUDIO AND VIDEO [S-16]

- Multimedia comes in many different formats like music, picture, sound, videos, records, films, animations, and more.
- Sometimes we need to add music or video into our web page. The easiest way to add video or sound to our web site is to include the special HTML tag called <embed>. This tag causes the browser itself to include controls for the multimedia automatically provided browser supports <embed> tag and given media type.

  Syntax: `<embed src=" "> …. </embed>`

- The <embed> tag defines a container for an external application or interactive content (a plug-in).

Attributes:

Attribute	Description
align	Determines how to align the object. It can be set to either center, left or right.
autostart	This boolean attribute indicates if the media should start automatically. We can set it either true or false.
loop	Specifies if the sound should be played continuously (set loop to true), a certain number of times (a positive value) or not at all (false)
playcount	Specifies the number of times to play the sound. This is alternate option for loop if we are using IE.
hidden	Specifies if the multimedia object should be shown on the page. A false value means no and true values means yes.
width	Width of the object in pixels
height	Height of the object in pixels
name	A name used to reference the object.
src	URL of the object to be embedded.
volume	Controls volume of the sound. Can be from 0 (off) to 100 (full volume).

- The <source> tag is used to specify multiple media resources for media elements, such as <video> and <audio>.

1. Audio:

- A sound file format is a file format for storing audio on a computer. There are several different formats like:

Format	File	Description
MIDI	.mid .midi	MIDI (Musical Instrument Digital Interface). Main format for all electronic music devices like synthesizers and PC sound cards. MIDI files do not contain sound, but digital notes that can be played by electronics. Plays well on all computers and music hardware, but not in web browsers.
RealAudio	.rm .ram	RealAudio. Developed by Real Media to allow streaming of audio with low bandwidths. Does not play in web browsers.
WMA	.wma	WMA (Windows Media Audio). Developed by Microsoft. Commonly used in music players. Plays well on Windows computers, but not in web browsers.
AAC	.aac	AAC (Advanced Audio Coding). Developed by Apple as the default format for iTunes. Plays well on Apple computers, but not in web browsers.

contd. ...

WAV	.wav	WAV. Developed by IBM and Microsoft. Plays well on Windows, Macintosh, and Linux operating systems. Supported by HTML5.
Ogg	.ogg	Ogg. Developed by the Xiph.Org Foundation. Supported by HTML5.
MP3	.mp3	MP3 files are actually the sound part of MPEG files. MP3 is the most popular format for music players. Combines good compression (small files) with high quality. Supported by all browsers.
MP4	.mp4	MP4 is a video format, but can also be used for audio. MP4 video is the upcoming video format on the internet. This leads to automatic support for MP4 audio by all browsers.

- HTML5 provides a standard for playing audio files. The <audio> tag defines sound, such as music or other audio streams. Before HTML5, audio files could only be played with a plug-in (like flash).

  Syntax: `<audio src=" ">......</audio>`

Example for audio files.

```
<!DOCTYPE html>
<html>
<body>
<audio controls>
   <source src="horse.ogg" type="audio/ogg">
   <source src="horse.mp3" type="audio/mpeg">
   Your browser does not support the audio element.
</audio>
</body>
</html>
```

Output:

- We can use HTML <bgsound> tag to play a soundtrack in the background of our web page. This tag is supported by Internet Explorer only and most of the other browsers ignore this tag. It downloads and plays an audio file when the host document is first downloaded by the user and displayed. The background sound file also will replay whenever the user refreshes the browser.

Example for <bgsound> tag.

```
<!DOCTYPE html>
<html>
<head>
<title>HTML embed Tag</title>
</head>
<body>
```

```
<bgsound src="/html/yourfile.mid">
<noembed><img src="yourimage.gif" ></noembed>
</bgsound>
</body>
</html>
```

2. Video:

- Before HTML5, there was no standard for showing videos on a web page. Before HTML5, videos could only be played with a plug-in (like flash).
- The HTML5 <video> element specifies a standard way to embed a video in a web page.

  Syntax: `<video src=" ">…..</video>`

Attributes:

- width and height: Define the dimensions of the playback-window, if not set the browser tries to use the dimensions from the video.
- loop: Sets the video to play in a loop.
- autoplay: Starts the video immediately.
- controls: Tells the browser to display a set of controls for playback, seeking and volume. Which controls these are and how they look depends on the browser.
- autobuffer: Automatically start buffering (loading) the video, so it's first loaded if we start playing. Currently Chrome and Safari ignore this attribute, so the video is being buffered on page load.
- poster: Here we can supply an image which will be displayed while the movie is not loaded yet.

Common Video Formats are given below:

Format	File	Description
MPEG	.mpg .mpeg	MPEG. Developed by the Moving Pictures Expert Group. The first popular video format on the web. Used to be supported by all browsers, but it is not supported in HTML5 (See MP4).
AVI	.avi	AVI (Audio Video Interleave), developed by Microsoft. Commonly used in video cameras and TV hardware. Plays well on Windows computers, but not in web browsers.
WMV	.wmv	WMV (Windows Media Video), developed by Microsoft. Commonly used in video cameras and TV hardware. Plays well on Windows computers, but not in web browsers.
QuickTime	.mov	QuickTime, developed by Apple. Commonly used in video cameras and TV hardware. Plays well on Apple computers, but not in web browsers.
RealVideo	.rm .ram	RealVideo, developed by Real Media to allow video streaming with low bandwidths. It is still used for online video and Internet TV, but does not play in web browsers.

contd. …

Flash	.swf .flv	Flash, developed by Macromedia. Often requires an extra component (plug-in) to play in web browsers.
Ogg	.ogg	Theora Ogg., developed by the Xiph.Org Foundation. Supported by HTML5.
WebM	.webm	WebM, developed by the web giants, Mozilla, Opera, Adobe, and Google. Supported by HTML5.
MPEG-4 or MP4	.mp4	MP4, developed by the Moving Pictures Expert Group. Based on QuickTime. Commonly used in newer video cameras and TV hardware. Supported by all HTML5 browsers. Recommended by YouTube.

Example for video files.

```
<!DOCTYPE html>
<html>
<body>
<video width="320" height="240" autoplay>
   <source src="movie1.mp4" type="video/mp4">
   <source src="movie1.bear" type="video/bear">
</video>
</body>
</html>
```

Output:

3.8 HTML FORMS AND FORM ELEMENTS [W-16, 17, S-17, 18]

- HTML forms are used to pass data to a server.
- A form is a group of controls that the user interacts with and sends the result to a specific files as designed by an application developer.
- To create an effective form, HTML provides various text based and selection controls that can handle almost any scenario. Besides these, there are action controls that actually send a signal to a script.
- A form is the central control that manages the other controls. Although the controls can send their data to a script, a form can be used to collect the values typed or selected on the controls, gather them as if they constituted one control and make these values available to a validating file on a server.

- A form can contain input elements like text fields, checkboxes, radio-buttons, submit buttons and more. A form can also contain select lists, textarea, fieldset, legend, and label elements.
- The <form> tag is used to create an HTML form for user input, like this

```
<form>
.
.
.
input elements
.
.
.
</form>
```

- HTML forms are required when we want to collect some data from the site visitor. For example: registration information: name, email address, credit card, etc.
- A simple syntax of using <form> is as follows:

```
<form action="back-end script" method="posting method">
form elements like input, textarea etc.
</form>
```

- Most frequently used form attributes are:
  1. **name:** This is the name of the form.
  2. **action:** Here we will specify any script URL which will receive uploaded data.
  3. **method:** Here we will specify method to be used to upload data. It can take various values but most frequently used are GET and POST.

     HTML documents are generally retrieved by requesting it's URL from web server using GET method. When large amount of data is to be passed to server. POST method is used. In POST, form contents are not send in URL. In POST method, form contents are send to server in the body of message.
  4. **target:** It specifies the target page where the result of the script will be displayed. It takes values like _blank, _self, _parent etc.
  5. **enctype:** We can use the enctype attribute to specify how the browser encodes the data before it sends it to the server. Possible values are like:
     - **application/x-www-form-urlencoded:** This is the standard method most forms use. It converts spaces to the plus sign and non-alphanumeric characters into the hexadecimal code for that character in ASCII text.
     - **mutlipart/form-data:** This allows the data to be sent in parts, with each consecutive part corresponding the a form control, in the order they appear in the form. Each part can have an optional content-type header of its own indicating the type of data for that form control.

- There are different types of form controls that we can use to collect data from a visitor to our site.
  - Text input controls.
  - Buttons.
  - Checkboxes and radio buttons.
  - Select boxes.
  - File select boxes.
  - Hidden controls.
  - Submit and reset button.

I. <input> Tag:

- The most important form element is the input tag.
- <input> defines an input control.
- The input tag is used to select user information.
- An input tag can vary in many ways, depending on the type attribute. An <input> tag can be of type text field, checkbox, password, radio button, submit button, and more.
- <input> tag are used within a <form> element to declare input controls that allow users to input data.
- An input field can vary in many ways, depending on the type attribute.

  Syntax: `<input type= " ">`
- Following is the list of attributes for <input> tag.
  1. **type:** Indicates the type of input control we want to create. This element is also used to create other form controls such as radio buttons and checkboxes.
  2. **name:** Used to give the name part of the name/value pair that is sent to the server, representing each form control and the value the user entered.
  3. **value:** Provides an initial value for the text input control that the user will see when the form loads.
  4. **size:** Allows us to specify the width of the text-input control in terms of characters.
  5. **maxlength:** Allows us to specify the maximum number of characters a user can enter into the text box.

1. Text Field:

- Text fields are one line areas that allow the user to input text.

  Syntax: `<input type = "text">`
- Following is the list of attributes for <input> tag.
  1. **type:** Indicates the type of input control we want to create. This element is also used to create other form controls such as radio buttons and checkboxes.
  2. **name:** Used to give the name part of the name/value pair that is sent to the server, representing each form control and the value the user entered.
  3. **value:** Provides an initial value for the text input control that the user will see when the form loads.

4. **size:** Allows us to specify the width of the text-input control in terms of characters.
5. **maxlength:** Allows us to specify the maximum number of characters a user can enter into the text box.

- Here, is a basic example of a single-line text input used to take first name and last name:

```
<!DOCTYPE html>
<body>
<head>
<title>Concepts of Form</title>
<form action="/cgi-bin/hello_get.cgi" method="get">
First name:
<input type="text" name="first_name" />
<br>
Last name:
<input type="text" name="last_name" />
<br>
<input type="submit" value="submit" />
</form>
</body>
</head>
</html>
```

Output:

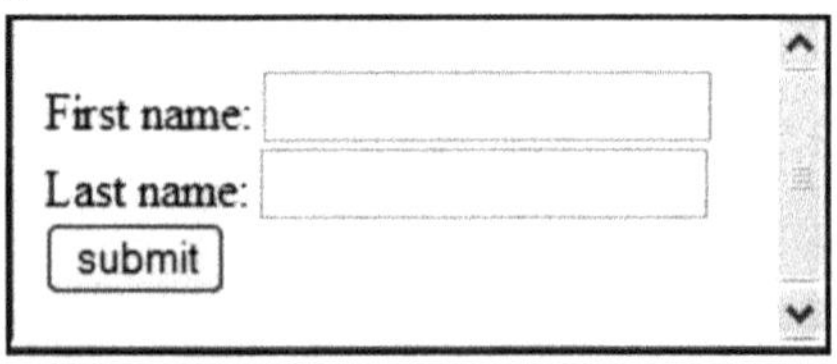

2. **Password Field:**

- Password fields are similar to text fields.
- The difference is that what is entered into a password field shows up a dots on the screen. This is, of course, to prevent others from reading the password on the screen.

Syntax: `<input type = "password">`

Attribute	Description
1. size=	Characters shown.
2. maxlength=	Max characters allowed.
3. name=	Name of the field.
4. value=	Initial value in the field.
5. align=	Alignment of the field.
6. tabindex=	Tab order of the field.

Example for password field.

```
<!DOCTYPE html>
<head>
<title>MyPage</title>
<head>
<body>
<form name="myform"
action="http://www.mydomain.com/myformhandler.cgi"
method="POST">
<div align="center">
Enter Password: <input type="password" size="25">
<br><br>
</div>
</form>
</body>
</html>
```

Output:

Enter Password: [ ]

3. Hidden Field:

- Hidden fields are similar to text fields. The difference is that the hidden field does not show on the page. Therefore the visitor cannot type anything into a hidden field, which leads to the purpose of the field. To submit information that is not entered by the visitor.

  Syntax: <input type = "hidden">

Attribute	Description
1. name=	Name of the field
2. value=	Value of the field

Example for hidden field.

```
<!DOCTYPE html>
<head>
<title>MyPage</title>
<head>
<body>
<form name="myform"
action="http://www.mydomain.com/myformhandler.cgi" method="POST">
<div align="center">
<input type="text" size="25" value="Enter your name here!">
<input type="hidden" name="Language" value="English">
```

```
<br><br>
</div>
</form>
</body>
<html>
```

Output:

Enter your name here!

- The hidden field does not show, but still, when the form is submitted the hidden field is sent with it.
- In above example, the hidden field would tell the program that handles the form, that the users preferred language in English.

4. Radio Buttons:

- Radio buttons are used when only one option is required to be selected. They are created using <input> tag.

  Syntax: `<input type="radio">`
- Following is the list of important radiobox attributes:
  1. type: Indicates that we want to create a radiobox.
  2. name: Name of the control.
  3. value: Used to indicate the value that will be sent to the server if this option is selected.
  4. checked: Indicates that this option should be selected by default when the page loads.

Example for radio button.

```
<!DOCTYPE html>
<head>
<title>Practice HTML input radiobox tag</title>
</head>
<body>
<form action="/cgi-bin/radiobutton.cgi" method="post">
<input type="radio" name="subject" value="maths" /> Maths
<input type="radio" name="subject" value="physics" /> Physics
<input type="submit" value="Select Subject" />
</form>
</body>
</html>
```

Output:

○ Maths ○ Physics [Select Subject]

5. Checkbox Control:

- Checkboxes are used when more than one option is required to be selected. They are created using <input> tag.

  Syntax: `<input type="checkbox">`
- Following is the list of important checkbox attributes:
  1. type: Indicates that we want to create a checkbox.
  2. name: Name of the control.
  3. value: The value that will be used if the checkbox is selected. More than one checkbox should share the same name only if we want to allow users to select several items from the same list.
  4. checked: Indicates that when the page loads, the checkbox should be selected.

Example for checkboxes.

```
<!DOCTYPE html>
<head>
<title>Practice HTML input checkbox tag</title>
</head>
<body>
<p>Try with different checkbox and different attributes</p>
<form action="" method="get">
<input type="checkbox" name="maths" value="on" /> Maths
<input type="checkbox" name="physics" value="on" /> Physics
<input type="reset" value="Select Subject" />
</form>
</body>
</html>
```

Output:

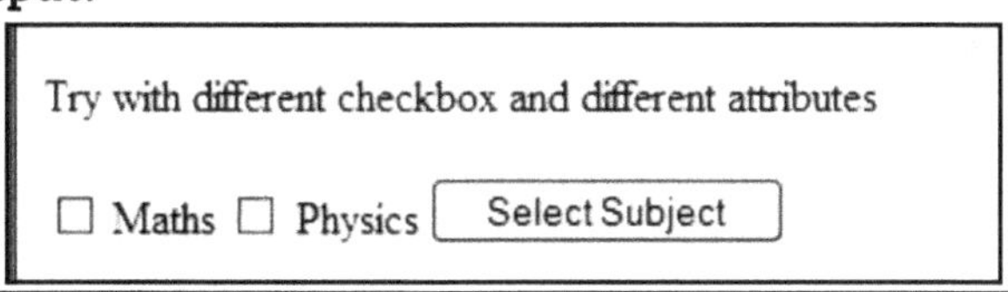

II. <label> Tag:

- The <label> tag defines a label for an <input> element.
- The <label> tag does not render as anything special for the user. However, it provides a usability improvement for mouse users, because if the user clicks on the text within the <label> element, it toggles the control.
- The for attribute of the <label> tag should be equal to the id attribute of the related element to bind them together.

III. <fieldset> Tag:

- <fieldset> Defines a border around elements in a form. The <fieldset> tag is used to group related elements in a form.
- The <fieldset> tag draws a box around the related elements.

IV. <textarea> Tag:

- It defines a multi-line text input control. Textarea are text fields that can span several lines.
- A textarea can hold an unlimited number of characters, and the text renders in a fixed-width font, (usually Courier).
- The size of a text area is specified by the cols and rows attributes.

  Syntax: `<textarea>.........</textarea>`
- Attributes for <textarea> tag are:
  1. name: The name of the control. This is used in the name/value pair that is sent to the server.
  2. rows: Indicates the number of rows of text area box.
  3. cols: Indicates the number of columns of text area box.

Example for <textarea> tag.

```
<!DOCTYPE html>
<body>
<head>
<title>Concepts of Form</title>
<p> This example cannot be edited because our editor uses a textarea for input, and your browser does not allow a textarea inside a textarea. </p>
<textarea rows="10" cols="30"> The cat was playing in the garden.
</textarea>
</body>
</head>
</html>
```

Output:

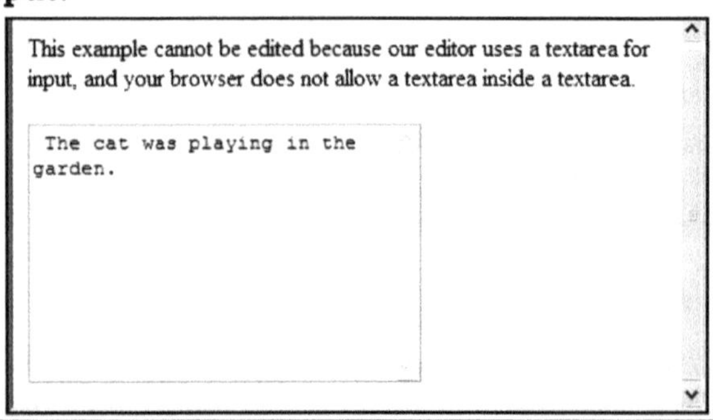

V. <select>Tag:

- The <select> tag is used to create a drop-down list.
- Drop-down list is used when we have many options available to be selected but only one or two will be selected.
- The <option> tags inside the <select> element define the available options in the list.

  Syntax: `<select>............</select>`

Attributes	Value	Description
1. disabled	disabled	This attribute specifies that a drop-down list should be disabled.
2. multiple	multiple	This attribute specifies that multiple options can be selected at once.
3. name	name	This attribute defines a name for the drop-down list.
4. size	number	This attribute specifies defines the number of visible options in a drop-down list.

Example for <select> tag.

```
<!DOCTYPE html>
<head>
<title>Practice HTML input selectbox tag</title>
</head>
<body>
<p>Try  with different selectbox and different attributes</p>
<form action="" method="get">
<select name="dropdown">
<option value="Maths" selected>Maths</option>
<option value="Physics">Physics</option>
</select>
<input type="reset" value="reset" />
</form>
</body>
</html>
```

Output:

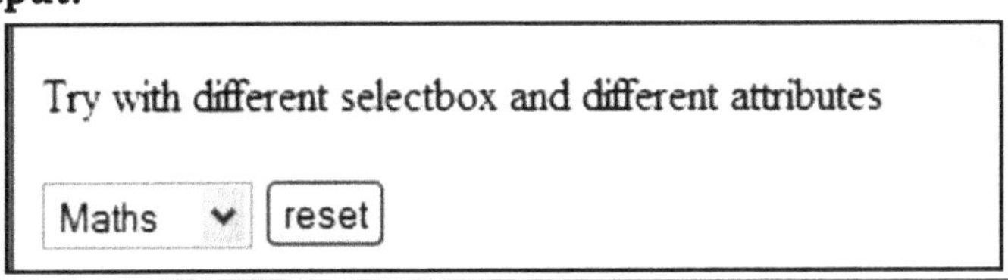

VI. Creating Button:

- The <button> tag defines a push button.
- There are various ways in HTML to create clickable buttons. We can create clickable button using <input> tag.
- When we use the <input> element to create a button, the type of button we create is specified using the type attribute.
- The type attribute can take the following values:
  1. **submit:** This creates a button that automatically submits a form.

2. **reset:** This creates a button that automatically resets form controls to their initial values.
3. **button:** This creates a button that is used to trigger a client-side script when the user clicks that button.

Syntax: <button>...............</button>

Attributes	Value	Description
1. disabled	disabled	This attribute specifies that a button should be disabled.
2. name	name	This attribute specifies the name for a button.
3. type	button reset submit	This attribute specifies the type of button.
4. value	text	This attribute specifies the initial value for a button.

Example for <button> tag.

```
<!DOCTYPE html>
<body>
<form name="input" action="html_form_action.asp" method="get">
First name: <input type="text" name="FirstName"
value="Mickey" /><br />
Last name: <input type="text" name="LastName" value="Mouse" /><br />
<input type="submit" value="Submit" />
</form>
<p>If you click the "Submit" button, the form-data will be sent to a
page called "html_form_action.asp".</p>
</body>
</html>
```

Output:

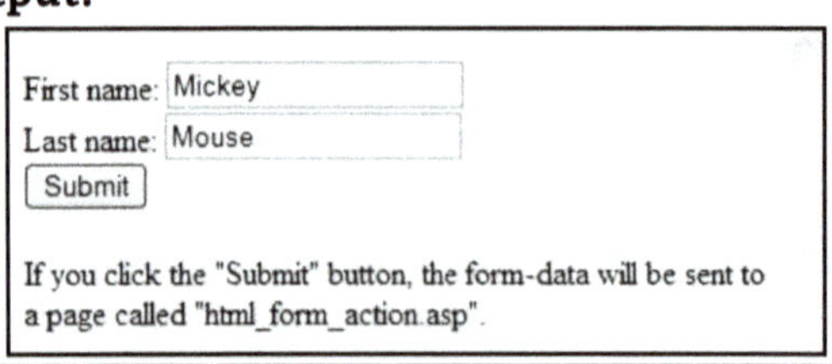

Example for submit and reset button.

```
<!DOCTYPE html>
<body>
<form action="/cgi-bin/hello_get.cgi" method="get">
First name:
<input type="text" name="first_name" />
<br>
```

```
Last name:
   <input type="text" name="last_name" />
   <input type="submit" value="Submit" />
   <input type="reset" value="Reset" />
</form>
</body>
</html>
```

Output:

VII.<option> Tag:

- It defines an option in a select list.
- The <option> tag go inside a <select> element.

Syntax: <option>..............</option>

Attributes	Value	Description
1. disabled	disabled	This attribute specifies that an option should be disabled.
2. label	text	This attribute specifies a shorter label for an option.
3. selected	selected	This attribute specifies that an option should be pre-selected when the page loads.
4. value	text	This attribute specifies the value to be sent to a server.

Example for <option> tag.

```
<!DOCTYPE html>
<body>
<form name="myform" action="nextpage.html" method="post" > <select size=1
name="mydropdown">
<option value="milk">Fresh Milk</option><br>
<option value="cheese">Old Cheese</option><br>
<option value="bread">Hot Bread</option>
</select>
</form>
</body>
</html>
```

Output:

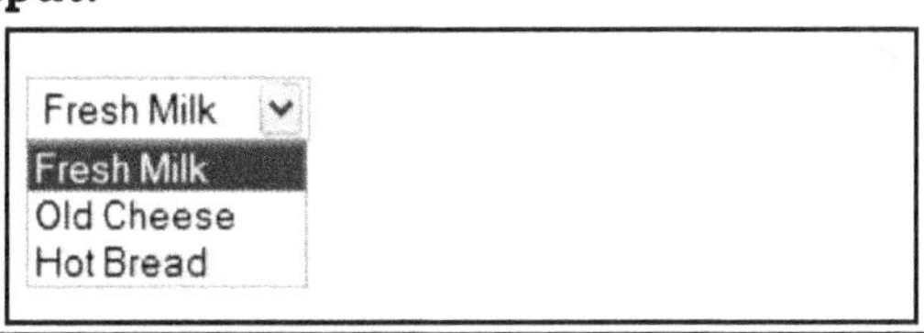

Example for form using various controls.

```
<!DOCTYPE html>
<body>
<head><h3><b> EX. FORM FOR RADIO BUTTON, CHECKBOXES & PULL DOWN
MENU</b></h3>
</head>
<form action="nextpage.html" method ="post">
<h3>Enter your information:</h3>
<b><i>Enter your name:</b>
<input type=text size="25"><br>
<b><i>Your age is in between:</b><br>
<input type="radio" name="radios" value="radio1" checked>15-20 yrs<br>
<input type="radio" name="radios" value="radio2">20-25 yrs<br>
<input type="radio" name="radios" value="radio3">25 yrs and
above<br>
<br><b><i>
Your Hobbies
<input type=checkbox name="option" value="read">Reading novels
<br>
<input type="checkbox" name="option" value="write" checked>
Writing <br>
<input type="checkbox" name="option" value="sing">Singing <br>
<br><br><b><i> Enter your city: </b>
<select>
<option value=pune> Pune </option>
<option value=mumbai> Mumbai</option>
<option value=a'nagar> Ahmednagar </option>
</select><br><br>
<input type="submit" name="button" value="Submit data">
</form>
</body>
</html>
```

Output:

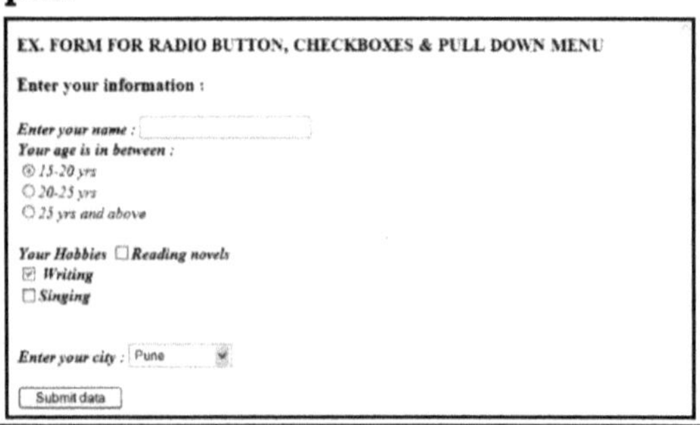

3.9 INTRODUCTION TO HTML FRONTPAGE

- Microsoft FrontPage is a discontinued WYSIWYG HTML editor and Web site administration tool from Microsoft for the Microsoft Windows line of operating systems.
- It was branded as part of the Microsoft Office suite from 1997 to 2003.
- Microsoft FrontPage has since been replaced by Microsoft Expression Web and SharePoint Designer, which were first released in December 2006 alongside Microsoft Office 2007.
- FrontPage, in its simplest form, is an HTML editor. That is the functionality upon which we'll focus in this section.
- Start a new FrontPage document, by clicking the FrontPage icon, , or by choosing FrontPage from Start : Programs (see Window below).]

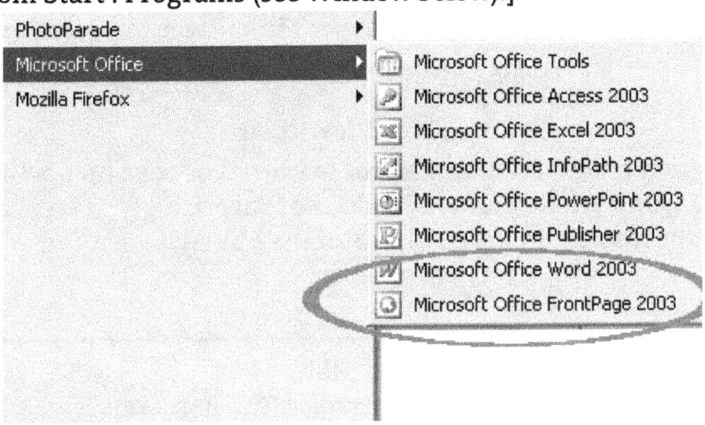

- We will see a new white page on which to begin creating our masterpiece! If we have already started a page, from the menu, choose FILE : Open and browse for the file that we want to work on.
- When we launch FrontPage, we see the basic program layout.
- This workspace is our control centre for creating websites and pages.
- FrontPage 2003 editing window looks like:

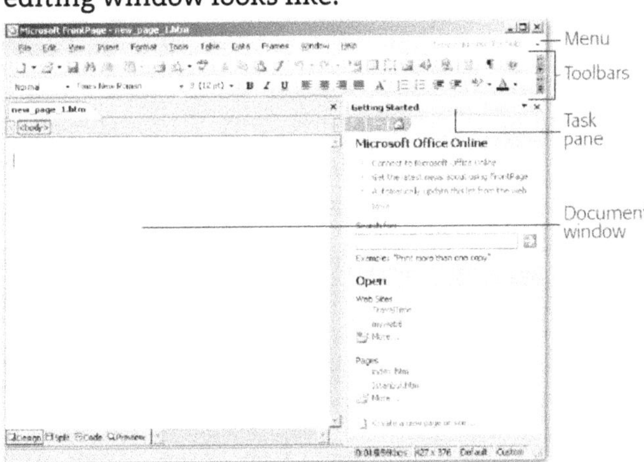

- Above Windows provides following comments:
  1. Two toolbars (standard and formatting) display the first time we open FrontPage. These two get top billing because they contain the most commonly used commands.
  2. The menu bar contains program commands. They follow the basic layout of Microsoft menus.
  3. The screen is dominated by the document window, in which we will do most of our work.
  4. The Design view in which we do our WYSIWYG work.
  5. The Split view that displays the HTML coding in a top window pane and the WYSIWYG view of our page in a bottom window pane.
  6. The Code view of the actual HTML coding the creates our page.
  7. The Preview view that we click when we want to test our document and view an approximation of the page as it will appear in the web browser.

FrontPage View Toolbar

  8. The program includes another helpful feature that pops up now and then looking to assist us with a whole bunch of tasks. Not surprisingly, it is called the task pane. The task pane display on the right side of the screen.

Summary

- HTML stands for HyperText Markup Language.
- HTML was invented in 1990 by a scientist called Tim Berners-Lee.
- HTML filenames are suffixed with .htm or .html extensions.
- Common HTML tags are <html>, <head>, <title>, <body> etc.
- Text formatting tags are <b>, <em>, <i>, <small>, <strong>, <sub>, <sup>, <ins>, <del>, <u>, <strike>, <big> etc.
- Block Level Tags: <!--...--> comment, HTML heading tags, <p>, <br>, <center>, <div>, <span>, <hr>, Marquees, <font> etc.
- There are two different views of markup, logical markup and physical markup. HTML has some logical tags and some physical tags.
- There are basically two types of graphic programs: Bitmap based and Vector based.
- The ismap attribute specifies that the image is part of a server-side image-map.
- The attributes ISMAP and USEMAP are basically used to give the server side and client side image maps.
- HTML gives us three different types of lists, i.e. an unordered list, an ordered list and a definition list
- An unordered list is a collection of related items that have no special order or sequence.

- The typical browser formats the contents of an ordered list just like an unordered list, except that the items are numbered instead of bulleted.
- A definition list is a list of items, with a description of each item.
- Tables are very useful to arrange in HTML and they are used very frequently by almost all web developers.
- Frames allow us to split the browser window into multiple windows that can display different pages. This will make the navigation much easier for the visitor.
- A sound file format is a file format for storing audio on a computer.
- The HTML5 <video> element specifies a standard way to embed a video in a web page.
- HTML forms are used to pass data to a server.
- Microsoft FrontPage is a discontinued WYSIWYG HTML editor and Web site administration tool from Microsoft for the Microsoft Windows line of operating systems.

Check Your Understanding

Multiple Choice Questions.

1. HTML is what type of language ?
   (a) Scripting Language (b) Markup Language
   (c) Programming Language (d) Network Protocol
2. The year in which HTML was first proposed ______.
   (a) 1990 (b) 1980
   (c) 2000 (d) 1995
3. Apart from <b> tag, what other tag makes text bold ?
   (a) <fat> (b) <strong>
   (c) <black> (d) <emp>
4. How can we make a bulleted list with numbers?
   (a) <dl> (b) <ol>
   (c) <list> (d) <ul>
5. What tag is used to display a picture in a HTML page?
   (a) picture (b) image
   (c) img (d) src
6. Which HTML tag produces the biggest heading?
   (a) <h7> (b) <h9>
   (c) <h4> (d) <h1>
7. HTML web pages can be read and rendered by ______.
   (a) Compiler (b) Server
   (c) Web Browser (d) Interpreter
8. Who is known as the father of World Wide Web (WWW)?
   (a) Robert Cailliau (b) Tim Thompson
   (c) Charles Darwin (d) Tim Berners-Lee

9. What should be the first tag in any HTML document?
   (a) <head> (b) <title>
   (c) <html> (d) <document>
10. HTML uses.......
   (a) User defined tags (b) Pre-specified tags
   (c) Fixed tags defined by the language (d) Tags only for linking

Answers

1. (a)	2. (c)	3. (c)	4. (c)	5. (b)	6. (b)	7. (a)	8. (b)	9. (d)	10. (a)

Practice Questions

Q.1 Answer the following Question in short.

1. What are the types of web pages?
2. Which four tags are required in every HTML page?
3. What is a form?
4. Write the basic structure of the HTML template?
5. What is Anchor tag and how can we open an URL into a new tab when clicked?

Q.2 Answer the following Question in detail.

1. How will we build a web site?
2. Distinguish between dynamic and static web pages.
3. Write and explain the steps to publish our page on the Internet.
4. How will we use different header tags in the HTML page?
5. Write HTML code to generate the following:
   - Left alignment for the sentence
     "This is my first web page"
   - Change the font from Arial to Courier new and write the sentence.
     "Now onwards I will try to write something useful for your people".
   - Insert proper Breaklines in the code.
6. Write the HTML codes for the following:
   I have
   - One car
   - One Motorcycle
   - One Bicycle

   I also have
   - One Bookshelf
   - One Computer
   - One CD-Player
7. How can we open a link in a new browser window?

8. Develop HTML code for the following:

   Go to the bottom

   –

   –

   Text for your article

   –

   Go to the top

9. Create a Email link to write a mail to your friend to invite him/her for your Birthday party, describing the venue, out and time.
10. Develop a web page to give information about your college.
11. Develop two web pages which will include questions and answers for different subjects and link to specific part from another document.
12. How can different types of images be used in the HTML code?
13. What is meant understand by client-side image map? Give one example.
14. Write a HTML code to generate the following output.

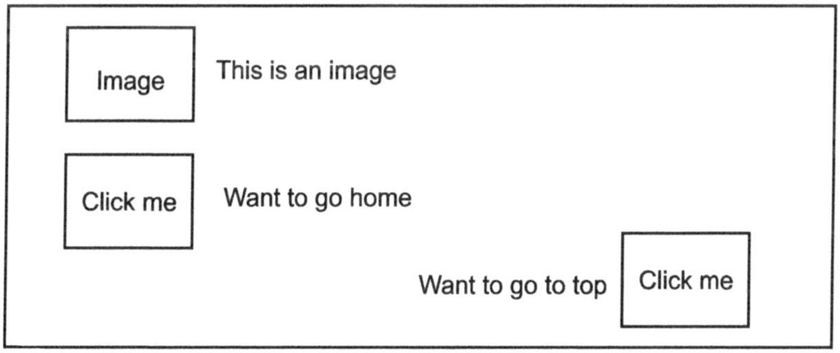

15. Explain why server-side image map is useful in HTML.
16. Write different types of image alignment and text wrapping formats.
17. What is a table? How do we build a table? What is the use of building a table?
18. Explain the different attributes that are used with <table> tag.
19. Write the HTML code to create the table shown in the following figure. (We can take any image).

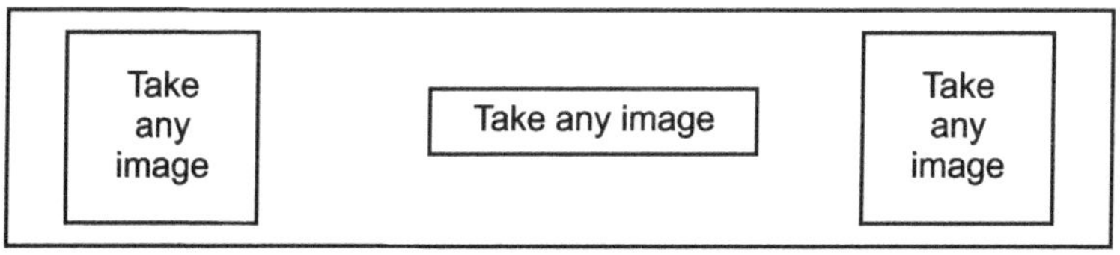

20. How do we create a frame? What is a frameset?
21. Explain different attributes that can be used with frame elements.

22. Write the HTML to list the name Mickey, Minnie, and Donald in a frame taking up the left 25 percent of the browser window. Make it so that clicking each name brings up a corresponding Web Page in the right 75 percent of the browser window.
23. How to create a form? Explain with example.
24. What are the methods used in forms.
25. Write code for following form:

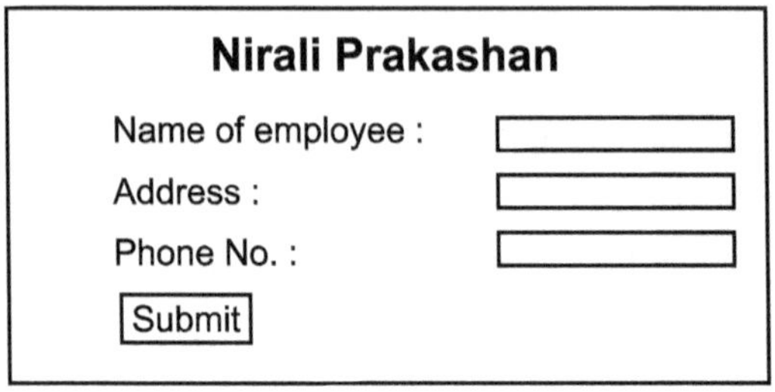

Q.3 Define the following terms.

1. Web page
2. Web publishing
3. Table
4. Frame
5. Physical HTML
6. Logical HTML
7. List
8. Embedding Audio
9. Embedding Video.

Previous Exams Questions

Summer 2019

1. Write any two attributes of <table> tag. **[2 M]**

Ans. Refer to Section 3.6.2.

2. Explain Marquee with two attributes **[2 M]**

Ans. Refer to Section 3.3.4.

3. Explain <pre> and <font> tag. **[2 M]**

Ans. Refer to Sections 3.3.3 and 3.3.4.

4. Explain the use of <frameset> tag with an example. **[4 M]**

Ans. Refer to Section 3.6.3.

5. Explain ordered and unordered list. **[4 M]**

Ans. Refer to Section 3.6.1.

6. How can user include images as hyperlink? Explain with example **[4 M]**

Ans. Refer to Section 3.5.

7. Write a HTML code to design the following table: **[4 M]**

Train Time Table			
TNO	**TNAME**	**Arrival Time**	**Departure Time**
101012	Nashik Express	2:00 pm	4:30 pm

Ans. Refer to Section 3.6.2.

8. Explain Embedding Audio, Video in HTML. **[4 M]**

Ans. Refer to Section 3.7.

Summer 2018

1. Give any two image mapping tags with example **[2 M]**

Ans. Refer to Section 3.5.

2. List any four tags used in HTML **[2 M]**

Ans. Refer to Section 3.3.

3. Explain in detail the various HTML frame tags. **[4 M]**

Ans. Refer to Section 3.6.3.

4. Write HTML code to design the following output for table: **[4 M]**

Train Time Table			
TNO	**TNAME**	**Arrival Time**	**Departure Time**
T01 T02	Rajdhani Indrayani	04:00 pm 05:15 pm	04:30 pm 05:45 pm

Ans. Refer to Section 3.6.2.

5. Explain HTML form elements with example. **[4 M]**

Ans. Refer to Section 3.8.

6. Write HTML and CSS code to design a web page. Divide the browser screen into two frames. The first frame will display the headings. Divide the second frame into two columns. Rightside frame containing "Home and kitchen appliances". Leftside frame contains details of appliances. **[4 M]**

Ans. Refer to Section 3.6.3.

7. Write short note on <div> and <span> tag. **[4 M]**

Ans. Refer to Section 3.3.4.

Winter 2017

1. Define <a> and <div> tag. **[2 M]**

Ans. Refer to Sections 3.3.5 and 3.3.4.

2. Define basic structure of HTML. **[2 M]**

Ans. Refer to Section 3.2.

3. Explain physical and logical tags in HTML. **[2 M]**

Ans. Refer to Section 3.4.

4. What is the use of <span> tag? **[2 M]**

Ans. Refer to Section 3.3.4.

5. Explain <pre> tag with example. **[2 M]**

Ans. Refer to Section 3.3.3.

6. Write HTML code to display the following frame: **[4 M]**

One		
two		**three**
four	five	six

Ans. Refer to Section 3.6.3.

7. What is Image Mapping? Explain its types. **[4 M]**

Ans. Refer to Section 3.5.

8. Write a HTML code to design the following table. **[4 M]**

Train Time Table			
TNO	**TNAME**	**Arrival Time**	**Departure Time**
101012	Nashik Express	2.00 pm	4.30 pm

Ans. Refer to Section 3.6.2.

9. Explain any two HTML form elements. **[4 M]**

Ans. Refer to Section 3.8.

10. Explain ordered and unordered list. **[4 M]**

Ans. Refer to Section 3.6.1.

Summer 2017

1. Explain <pre> tag with example. **[2 M]**

Ans. Refer to Section 3.3.3.

2. Explain <font> tag with two attributes. **[2 M]**

Ans. Refer to Section 3.3.

3. Explain <a> and <div> tags. **[2 M]**

Ans. Refer to Sections 3.3.5 and 3.3.4.

4. Write HTML code to design following output for table: **[4 M]**

Supplier Name	**Product Name**	**Product Details**		**Total Price**
		Price	**Quantity**	
Poonam Electronics	Printers	2500	08	20000
Raj Electronics	Scanner	1800	05	9000

Ans. Refer to Section 3.6.2.

5. Explain the use of <frameset> tag with an example. **[4 M]**

Ans. Refer to Section 3.6.3.

6. Explain ordered and unordered list. **[4 M]**

Ans. Refer to Section 3.6.1.

7. Explain any two HTML form elements. **[4 M]**

Ans. Refer to Section 3.8.

8. Write HTML code to design the following output frame: **[4 M]**

BCA	
TYBCA	Java Web tech OOPS Net

Ans. Refer to Section 3.6.2.

9. How can user include Image as Hyperlink? Explain with example. **[4 M]**

Ans. Refer to Section 3.5.

Winter 2016

1. What is the use of <span>? **[2 M]**

Ans. Refer to Section 3.3.4.

2. Explain <Font> Tag with two attributes. **[2 M]**

Ans. Refer to Section 3.3.4.

3. Define Basic structure of HTML. **[2 M]**

Ans. Refer to Section 3.2.

4. Explain Image Mapping and its type with example. **[4 M]**

Ans. Refer to Section 3.5.

5. Write HTML code to design the following output for table: **[4 M]**

Train Time-Table			
TNO	**TName**	**Arrival Time**	**Departure Time**
T0001	Mumbai Express	2:00 PM	2:30 PM

Ans. Refer to Section 3.6.2.

6. Explain Ordered and Unorder List. **[4 M]**

Ans. Refer to Section 3.6.1.

7. Explain <frames> Tag with example. **[4 M]**

Ans. Refer to Section 3.6.3.

8. Explain any two HTML form elements. **[4 M]**

Ans. Refer to Section 3.8.

9. Write HTML code to design the following output frame: **[4 M]**

<table>
<tr><th colspan="2">BCA</th></tr>
<tr><td>TYBCA</td><td>Java
Web tech
OOPS
Net</td></tr>
</table>

Ans. Refer to Section 3.6.2.

Summer 2016

1. Explain Marquee with two attributes. **[2 M]**

Ans. Refer to Section 3.3.4.

2. Give any two text formatting tags. **[2 M]**

Ans. Refer to Section 3.3.2.

3. Write HTML Code to create the following frame: **[4 M]**

<table>
<tr><td> </td><td> </td></tr>
<tr><td> </td><td> </td></tr>
<tr><td colspan="2"> </td></tr>
</table>

Ans. Refer to Section 3.6.3.

4. Explain image mapping. **[4 M]**

Ans. Refer to Section 3.5.

5. Write a HTML Code which generates the following output: **[4 M]**

1. Fruits:
    - Mango
    - Apple
    - Orange
2. Vegetables:
    - Tomato
    - Potato
    - Onion

Ans. Refer to Section 3.6.1.

6. Explain physical tags used in HTML. **[4 M]**

Ans. Refer to Section 3.4.

7. Explain Embedding Audio, Video in HTML. **[4 M]**

Ans. Refer to Section 3.7.

4...

Style Sheets

Objectives...

- To understand the need for CSS.
- To learn basic syntax and structure of CSS.
- To learn and implement CSS.
- To get the overview and features of CSS2 and CSS3.

4.1 INTRODUCTION

- In early days when web pages were formatted, developers were using markup elements.
- In the past, developers had few options to focus on the look or presentation of the web page.
- Mostly the markup elements provided by the HTML focuses on the structure of the data but not the presentation. Because of this there was a need to have a technology that could help the web developers to focus more on the presentation.
- Cascading Style Sheets got introduced in late 1996 and CSS provided more control over the layout, which helped the web developers.
- Introduction of CSS provided good level of separation on use of markup elements for structuring web page and their use for style or presentation of web page.
- The distinct division of duties between markup and style can provided numerous production, maintenance, and even performance benefits, making it a far superior presentation solution to markup alone.

4.2 NEED FOR CSS

- Cascading Style Sheet i.e. CSS is the language which is designed with the intension to present the content for making the web pages more presentable.
- Before CSS came into existence, HTML was the only major language in use to design the web pages.
- HTML had some limitations to make the web pages more presentable. For example if we use four different tables in a web page, and if wish to make them look more presentable, designers needed to repeat the same code for all the tables in HTML.
- HTML was designed with the intension to describe the content and not to present the content.

- CSS allows the designers to develop more styles better in presentation independent of HTML and once written can be applied on multiple markups without re-writing the code.
- There was need in division of duties of describing the content and presenting the content so as to help developers by minimizing the scope of thinking while designing the web page.

4.2.1 Introduction to CSS [S-16]

- Cascading Style Sheets is used to define styles for our web pages, including the design, layout and variations in display for different devices and screen sizes.
- CSS handles the look and feel part of a web page. Using CSS, we can control the color of the text, the style of fonts, the spacing between paragraphs, how columns are sized and laid out, what background images or colors are used, layout designs, variations in display for different devices and screen sizes as well as a variety of other effects.
- CSS is easy to learn and understand but it provides powerful control over the presentation of an HTML document. Most commonly, CSS is combined with the markup languages HTML or XHTML.
- CSS saves a lot of work. It can control the layout of multiple web pages all at once.
- Initially there was less response and interest to build CSS and CSS1 was launched in late 1996. But next version of CSS i.e. CSS2 was quite quickly launched in 1998.
- Though CSS was very helpful to the web designers it has less acceptance across the world as we had some problems from the various browsers. Many browsers those days was unable to provide support to CSS. This resulted in less use of CSS. Later the newer versions of the browsers were able to support the CSS features and succeeded in almost all the tests of CSS.

Advantages of CSS: [S-18]

1. **CSS saves time:** We can write CSS once and then reuse same sheet in multiple HTML pages. We can define a style for each HTML element and apply it to as many web pages as we want.
2. **Pages load faster:** If we are using CSS, we do not need to write HTML tag attributes every time. Just write one CSS rule of a tag and apply to all the occurrences of that tag. So less code means faster download times.
3. **Easy maintenance:** To make a global change, simply change the style, and all elements in all the web pages will be updated automatically.
4. **Superior styles to HTML:** CSS has a much wider array of attributes than HTML so we can give far better look to our HTML page in comparison of HTML attributes.
5. **Multiple Device Compatibility:** Style sheets allow content to be optimized for more than one type of device. By using the same HTML document, different versions of a web site can be presented for handheld devices such as PDAs and cell phones or for printing.
6. **Global web standards:** Now HTML attributes are being deprecated and it is being recommended to use CSS. So its a good idea to start using CSS in all the HTML pages to make them compatible to future browsers.

4.3 BASIC SYNTAX AND STRUCTURE [S-19, 18]

Concept of CSS

- Cascading style sheets are used to specify particular styles for a character, a word, a group of words, a page or a whole web site. Although we can change almost any behavior using these styles, including some behaviors that were not possible in HTML.
- CSS does not constitute an independent or complete language, the styles are used to control the display of items or sections on a web page.
- A CSS comprises of style rules that are interpreted by the browser and then applied to the corresponding elements in our document.
- A style rule is made of three parts:
  1. **Selector:** A selector is an HTML tag at which style will be applied. This could be any tag like <h1> or <table> etc.
  2. **Property:** A property is a type of attribute of HTML tag. Put simply, all the HTML attributes are converted into CSS properties. They could be color or border etc.
  3. **Value:** Values are assigned to properties. For example color property can have value either red or #F1F1F1 etc.
- **Syntax of CSS is:** `selector { property: value }`
- **Example:** We can define a table border as follows:

```
table{ border:1px solid #C00; }
```

Here, table is a selector and border is a property and given value 1px solid #C00 is the value of that property.

Type of Selectors:

- We can define selectors in various simple ways based on our comfort. Let me put these selectors one by one.

1. **Universal Selectors:**

Rather than selecting elements of a specific type, the universal selector quite simply matches the name of any element type:

```
* {
  color: #000000;
  }
```

This rule renders the content of every element in our document in black.

2. **Descendant Selectors:**

Suppose we want to apply a style rule to a particular element only when it lies inside a particular element. As given in the following example, style rule will apply to <em> element only when it lies inside <ul> tag.

```
ul em {
  color: #000000;
}
```

3. Class Selectors:

We can define style rules based on the class attribute of the elements. All the elements having that class will be formatted according to the defined rule. It is denoted by . (dot).

```
.black {
  color: #000000;
}
```

This rule renders the content in black for every element with class attribute set to black in our document. We can make it a bit more particular. For example:

```
h1.black {
  color: #000000;
}
```

This rule renders the content in black for only <h1> elements with class attribute set to black.

We can apply more than one class selectors to given element. Consider the following example:

```
<p class="center bold">
This para will be styled by the classes center and bold.
</p>
```

4. ID Selectors:

We can define style rules based on the id attribute of the elements. All the elements having that id will be formatted according to the defined rule.

```
#black {
  color: #000000;
}
```

This rule renders the content in black for every element with id attribute set to black in our document. We can make it a bit more particular. For example:

```
h1#black {
  color: #000000;
}
```

This rule renders the content in black for only <h1> elements with id attribute set to black. The true power of id selectors is when they are used as the foundation for descendant selectors, For example:

```
#black h2 {
  color: #000000;
}
```

In above example all level 2 headings will be displayed in black color only when those headings will lie within tags having id attribute set to black.

5. Child Selectors:

We have seen descendant selectors. There is one more type of selectors which is very similar to descendants but have different functionality. Consider the following example:

```
body > p {
  color: #000000;
}
```

This rule will render all the paragraphs in black if they are direct child of <body> element. Other paragraphs put inside other elements like <div> or <td> etc. would not have any effect of this rule.

6. Attribute Selectors:

We can also apply styles to HTML elements with particular attributes. The style rule below will match all input elements that has a type attribute with a value of text:

```
input[type="text"]{
  color: #000000;
}
```

The advantage to this method is that the <input type="submit" /> element is unaffected, and the color applied only to the desired text fields.

There are following rules applied to attribute selector.

- **p[lang]:** Selects all paragraph elements with a lang attribute.
- **p[lang="fr"]:** Selects all paragraph elements whose lang attribute has a value of exactly "fr".
- **p[lang~="fr"]:** Selects all paragraph elements whose lang attribute contains the word "fr".
- **p[lang|="en"]:** Selects all paragraph elements whose lang attribute contains values that are exactly "en", or begin with "en-".

7. Grouping Selectors:

We can apply a style to many selectors if we like. Just separate the selectors with a comma as given in the following example:

```
h1, h2, h3 {
color: #36C;
font-weight: normal;
letter-spacing: .4em;
margin-bottom: 1em;
text-transform: lowercase;
}
```

This define style rule will be applicable to h1, h2 and h3 element as well. The order of the list is irrelevant. All the elements in the selector will have the corresponding declarations applied to them.

We can combine various class selectors together as shown below:

```
#content, #footer, #supplement {
position: absolute;
left: 510px;
width: 200px;
}
```

Multiple Style Rules:

- We may need to define multiple style rules for a single element. We can define these rules to combine multiple properties and corresponding values into a single block as defined in the following example:

```
h1 {
color: #36C;
font-weight: normal;
letter-spacing: .4em;
margin-bottom: 1em;
text-transform: lowercase;
}
```

- Here, all the property and value pairs are separated by a semicolon (;). We can keep them in a single line or multiple lines. For better readability we keep them into separate lines.
- For a while do not bother about the properties mentioned in the above block.

4.4 TYPES OF STYLE SHEETS [S-17, W-17]

- CSS can be inserted in three following ways:
  1. Inline,
  2. Embedded(Internally),
  3. Externally.

4.4.1 Inline CSS

- An inline style loses many of the advantages of style sheets by mixing content with presentation.
- It is possible to place CSS right in the opening tag of HTML element.

Syntax:

```
<tag style="property1: value; property2: value;">
</tag>
```

Example for inline CSS.

```
<!DOCTYPE html>
<body>
<p style="background: pink; color: blue;">
Text color is green with blue background
</p>
</body>
</html>
```

Output:

```
Text color is green with blue background
```

4.4.2 Embedded (Internal) CSS

- An Internal style sheet should be used when a single document has a unique style.
- CSS can be inserted in HTML within the head section of HTML code. This is sometimes called embedding CSS in HTML.
- CSS and HTML are different, so we need to tell the browser that we are dealing with CSS. This is done using style tag followed by type attribute.

Syntax:

```
<head>
<style type="text/css">
selector { property: value; }
</style>
</head>
```

Example for Internal/Embedded Style sheet.

```
<!DOCTYPE html>
<head>
<style type="text/css">
p {
color: blue;
}
h1 {
color: red;
text-align: center;
}
body {
background-color: grey;
}
</style>
</head>
<body>
<h1>Internal CSS Example</h1>
<p> Now thats how CSS is inserted internally </p>
</body>
</html>
```

Output:

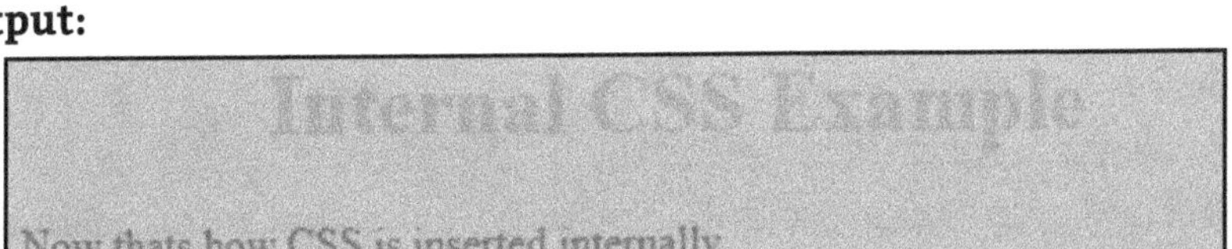

- In the above example, we inserted CSS code in the head section, using style tag. This tells the browser that the code that follows will be style sheet code.
  - **Paragraph** text will be blue in color.
  - **heading (h1)** will be center aligned and text color will be red.
  - **body** background color will be grey.

4.4.3 External CSS

- An external style sheet is ideal when the style is applied to many pages. With an external style sheet, we change the look of an entire web site by changing one file.
- Best way to insert CSS code is to write it in a different file and then refer it in HTML code.
- External CSS contains only CSS code and is saved with a ".css" file extension. This CSS file is referred from HTML file using the <link> tag.
- An external CSS is ideal when the style is applied to many web pages. Web designers can change the look of an entire web site by changing one file.

CSS Code:

```
p {
text-align: center;
color: white;
}
body {
background-color: green;
}
```

- Save the above file as sample.css

HTML Code:

```
<!DOCTYPE html>
<head>
<link rel="stylesheet" type="text/css" href="sample.css" />
</head>
<body>
<p> This is an example for inserting CSS externally. </p>
</body>
</html>
```

Output:

This is an example for inserting CSS externally.

4.5 USING CSS

1. **Background Properties:**

- The CSS background properties are used to define the background effects.
- The background properties are: background, background color, background image, background repeat, background position and background attachment.

Example for CSS background property.

```
<!DOCTYPE html>
<head>
<style type="text/css">
body { background: pink; }
</style>
</head>
<body>
This is an example for background
</body>
</html>
```

Output:

This is an example for background

(i) CSS Background color:

- We can specify a color for the background of an element using the background-color property like this,

```
background-color: value;
```

- Value could be color name, hexadecimal number or RGB color code.

Example for CSS background color.

```
<!DOCTYPE html>
<head>
<style type="text/css">
body { background-color: #DEB887; }
</style>
</head>
<body>
This is an example for background color with a hexadecimal number
</body>
</html>
```

Output:

This is an example for background color with a hexadecimal number

(ii) CSS Background image:

- We can set an image in the background using the background-image property.

Example for CSS background image.

```
<!DOCTYPE html>
<head>
<style type="text/css">
p { background-image: url(imageBG.gif); }
</style>
```

```
</head>
<body>
<p>This is a paragraph, and its background is an image.</p>
</body>
</html>
```

Output:

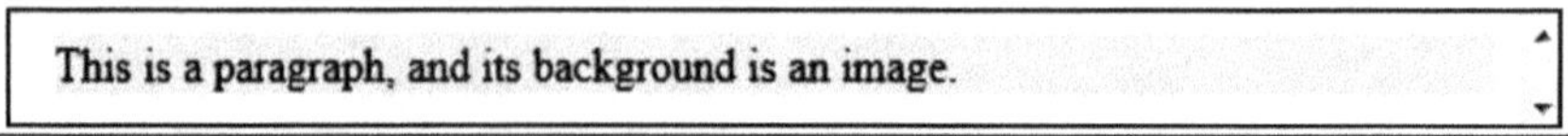

(iii) CSS Background position:

- We can position an image using background-position property like this,

```
background-position: value;
```

- Values could be top left, top center, top right, center left, center center, center right, bottom left, bottom center, bottom right, x% y% or x-pos y-pos.

Example for CSS background position.

```
<!DOCTYPE html>
<head>
<style type="text/css">
h1 {
background-image: url(geniusAtWork.gif);
background-position: top center;
}
h2 {
background-image: url(geniusAtWork.gif);
background-position: 30% 30%;
}
</style>
</head>
<body>
<h1>See the difference in image</h1>
<h2>See the difference in image</h2>
</body>
</html>
```

Output:

(iv) CSS Background Repeat:

- We can repeat the image set as a background using the background-repeat property like this,

```
background-repeat: value;
```

- Value could be no-repeat, repeat, repeat-x or repeat-y.

Example for background repeat.

```
<!DOCTYPE html>
<head>
<style type="text/css">
h1 {
background-image: url(geniusAtWork.gif);
background-position: repeat;
}
h2 {
background-image: url(geniusAtWork.gif);
background-repeat: repeat-y;
}
</style>
</head>
<body>
<h1>example for background repeat</h1>
<h2>example for background repeat</h2>
</body>
</html>
```

Output:

(v) CSS Background Attachment:

- We can set the image in background to scroll with the page or set it fixed when the user scrolls down the page using background-attachment property like this.

```
background-attachment: value;
```

- Value could be fixed or scroll.

Example for CSS background attachment.

```
<!DOCTYPE html>
<head>
<style type="text/css">
body
{
background-image: url('geniusAtWork.gif');
```

```
background-repeat: no-repeat;
background-attachment: fixed;
}
</style>
</head>
<body>
<p>An interesting story comes here. See example to read the story</p>
</body>
</html>
```

2. CSS Font Properties:

- We can change the text size, color, style, make it bold or light etc. using CSS font properties.
- The font properties are: font-family, font-size, font-weight, font-style and font-variant.

(i) CSS font family

- We can set the font to be serif, sans-serif, verdana, cursive etc. using font-family property like this,

```
font-family: value;
```

Example for CSS font family.

```
<!DOCTYPE html>
<head>
<style type="text/css">
h1 { font-family: serif; }
h2 { font-family: sans-serif; }
h3 { font-family: cursive; }
</style>
</head>
<body>
<h1>This is serif </h1>
<h2>This is sans-serif </h2>
<h3>This is cursive </h3>
</body>
</html>
```

Output:

(ii) CSS font size:

- We can set the font size using font-size property like this,

```
font-size: value;
```

- The value could be xx-large, px (pixel>, x-large, larger, large, medium, small, smaller, x-small, xx-small, length or %.

Example for CSS font size.

```
<!DOCTYPE html>
<head>
<style type="text/css">
p.first { font-size: 150%; }
p.second { font-size: 30px; }
p.third { font-size: small; }
</style>
</head>
<body>
<p class="first">This font is 150% </p>
<p class="second">This font is 30 pixels</p>
<p class="third">This font is small</p>
</body>
</html>
```

Output:

(iii) CSS font weight:

- We can make font thick or bold using the font-weight property like this,

```
font-weight: value;
```

- The value could be normal, bold, bolder, lighter or any number(usually multiples of 100 are used).

Example for CSS font weight.

```
<!DOCTYPE html>
<head>
<style type="text/css">
p.first { font-weight: normal; }
p.second { font-weight: bolder; }
```

```
p.third { font-weight: 900; }
</style>
</head>
<body>
<p class="first">This font is normal </p>
<p class="second">This font is bolder </p>
<p class="third">This font weight is 900</p>
</body>
</html>
```

Output:

This font is normal

This font is bolder

This font weight is 900

(iv) CSS font style:

- We can set font style using the font-style property like this,

```
font-style: value;
```

- The value could be normal, italic or oblique.

Example for CSS font style.

```
<!DOCTYPE html>
<head>
<style type="text/css">
p.first { font-style: normal; }
p.second { font-style: italic; }
p.third { font-style: oblique; }
</style>
</head>
<body>
<p class="first">This font is normal </p>
<p class="second">This font is italic </p>
<p class="third">This font is oblique</p>
</body>
</html>
```

Output:

This font is normal

This font is italic

This font is oblique

(v) CSS font variant:

- We can set font variant using the font-variant property like this,

```
font-variant: value;
```

- The value could be normal or small-caps.

Example for CSS font variant.

```
<!DOCTYPE html>
<head>
<style type="text/css">
p.first { font-variant: normal; }
p.second { font-variant: small-caps; }
</style>
</head>
<body>
<p class="first">This font is normal</p>
<p class="second">THIS FONT IS SMALLCAPS </p>
</body>
</html>
```

Output:

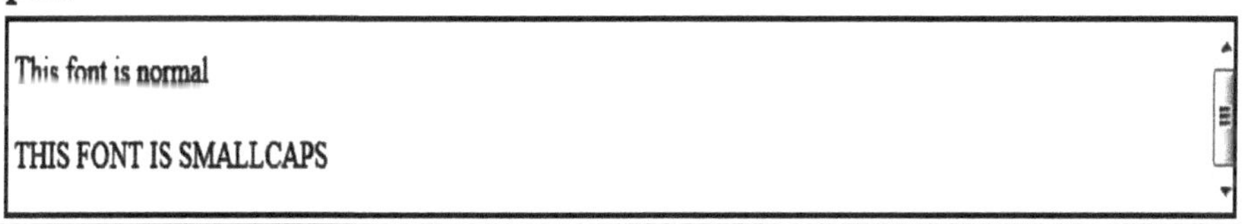

3. CSS text Properties: [S-16]

- Using CSS text properties we can control the text spacing, decoration, alignment or transform the text to upper or lowercase.
- The text properties are letter spacing, text decoration, text align, text transform, word spacing, text indent.

(i) CSS letter spacing:

- We can adjust the space between letters using letter spacing property.

  Syntax: `letter-spacing: value;`

  value could be normal or length (0.2ex, 0.3ex, 5ex, 1px etc).

Example for CSS letter spacing.

```
<!DOCTYPE html>
<head>
<style type="text/css">
p.first { letter-spacing: 5ex; }
p.second{ letter-spacing: normal; }
p.third { letter-spacing: 2px; }
</style>
```

```
</head>
<body>
<p class="first">Letter spacing is 5ex</p>
<p class="second">Letter spacing is normal </p>
<p class="third">Letter spacing is 2px </p>
</body>
</html>
```

Output:

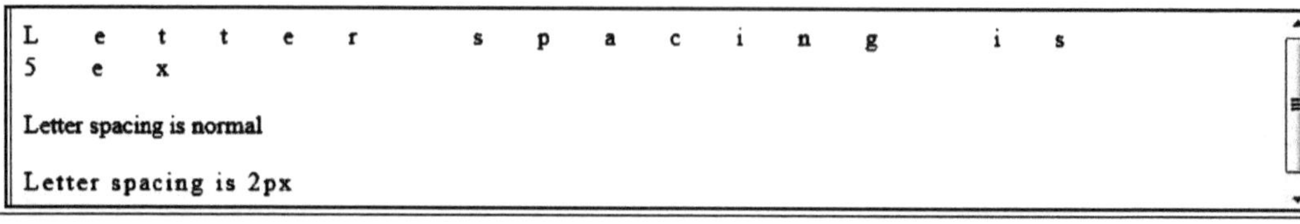

(ii) CSS text decoration:

- We can decorate the text using text decoration property.

  Syntax: `text-decoration: value;`

  value could be underline, overline, line through or blink

Example for CSS text decoration.

```
<!DOCTYPE html>
<head>
<style type="text/css">
p.first { text-decoration: underline; }
p.second{ text-decoration: line-through; }
p.third { text-decoration: overline; }
</style>
</head>
<body>
<p class="first">Text is underlined</p>
<p class="second">Text is lined-through </p>
<p class="third">Text is overlined </p>
</body>
</html>
```

Output:

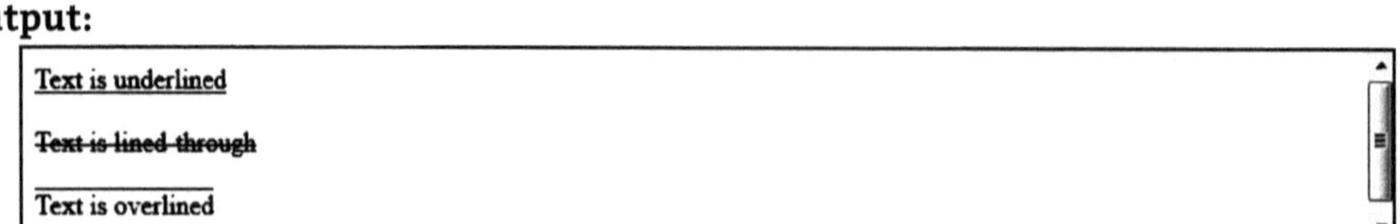

(iii) CSS text align:

- We can align the text using text align property.

  Syntax: `text-align: value;`

  value could be left, right, center or justify.

Example for CSS text align.

```
<!DOCTYPE html>
<head>
<style type="text/css">
p.first { text-align: center; }
p.second{ text-align: right; }
p.third { text-align: left; }
p.fourth{ text-align: justify; }
</style>
</head>
<body>
<p class="first">Text is centered</p>
<p class="second">Text is right aligned </p>
<p class="third">Text is left aligned </p>
<p class="fourth">Text is justified </p>
</body>
</html>
```

Output:

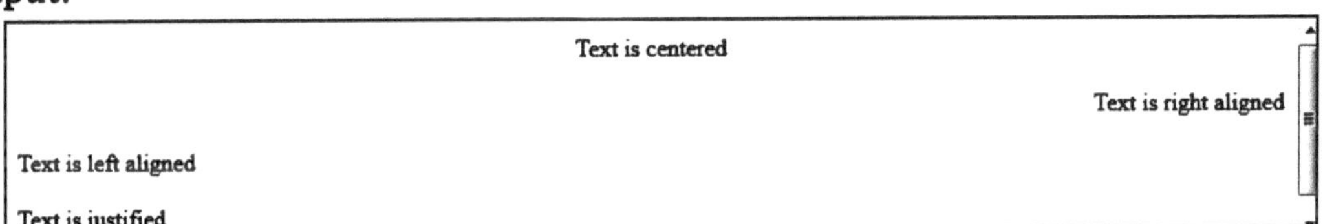

(iv) CSS text transform:

- We can transform the text to lowercase, uppercase or capitalize using text transform property.

  Syntax: `text-transform: value;`

  value could be capitalize, uppercase, or lowercase.

Example for CSS text transform.

```
<!DOCTYPE html>
<head>
<style type="text/css">
p.first { text-transform: capitalize; }
p.second{ text-transform: uppercase; }
p.third { text-transform: lowercase; }
</style>
</head>
<body>
<p class="first">This Text Is Capitalize</p>
<p class="second">this text uppercase </p>
<p class="third">THIS TEXT IS LOWERCASE </p>
</body>
</html>
```

Output:

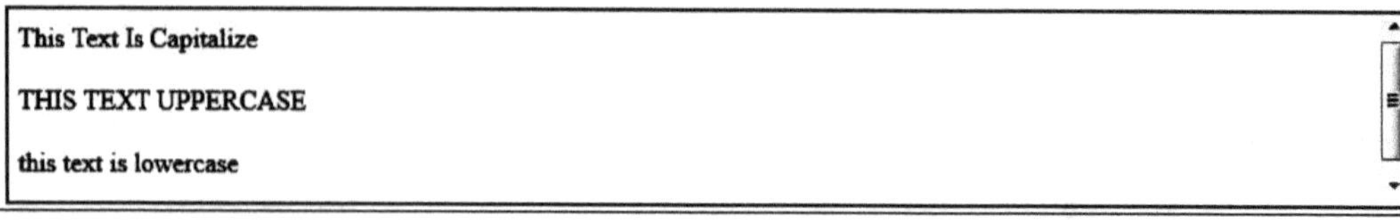

(v) CSS word spacing:

- We can adjust the spaces between words using word spacing property.

  Syntax: `word-spacing: value;`

  value could be normal, or value (0.2ex, 0.3ex, 5ex, 1px etc).

Example for CSS word spacing.

```
<!DOCTYPE html>
<head>
<style type="text/css">
h1 { word-spacing: normal; }
p{ word-spacing: 8px; }
</style>
</head>
<body>
<h1>Heading is normal</h1>
<p>This text has 8px space between words </p>
</body>
</html>
```

Output:

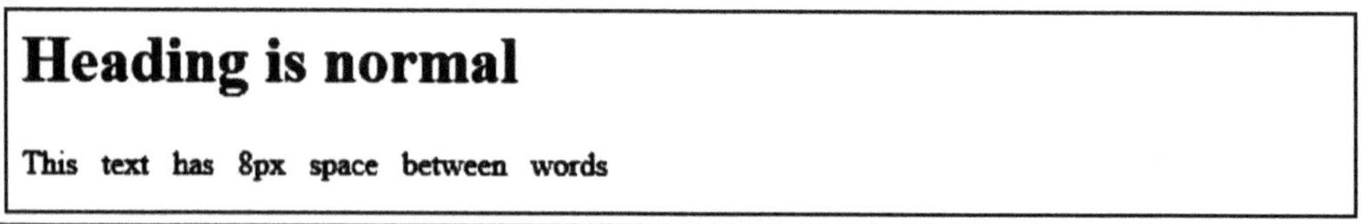

(vi) CSS text indent:

- We can indent the text using text indent property.

  Syntax: `text-indent: value;`

  value could be length like 1cm, 2em, 5px etc. or percentage like 20%, 30% etc.

Example for CSS text indent.

```
<!DOCTYPE html>
<head>
<style type="text/css">
h1 { text-indent: 50%; }
p{ text-indent: 50px; }
</style>
</head>
```

```
<body>
<h1>Heading is 50% intended</h1>
<p>You've got to start with the customer experience and work back towards
the technology - not the other way around.</p>
</body>
</html>
```

Output:

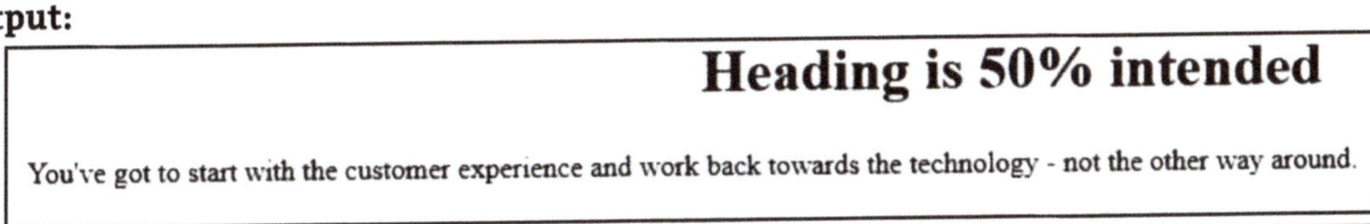

4. CSS border properties: [S-16]

- CSS border properties allow us to customize the borders.
- The border properties are: border style, border color, border width, border top, border bottom, border left and border right.

(i) CSS border style:

- We can style the borders of HTML elements using the border-style property.

  Syntax: `border-style: value;`

  value could be dashed, dotted, double, groove, hidden, inset, outset, ridge or solid.

Example for CSS border style.

```
<!DOCTYPE html>
<head>
<style type="text/css">
table.first { border-style: solid; }
table.second { border-style: dotted; }
table.third { border-style: inset; }
</style>
</head>
<body>
<table class="first">
<tr><td> Table is solid </td></tr>
</table><br/>
<table class="second">
<tr><td> Table is dotted </td></tr>
</table><br/>
<table class="third">
<tr><td> Table is inset </td></tr>
</table><br/>
</body>
</html>
```

Output:

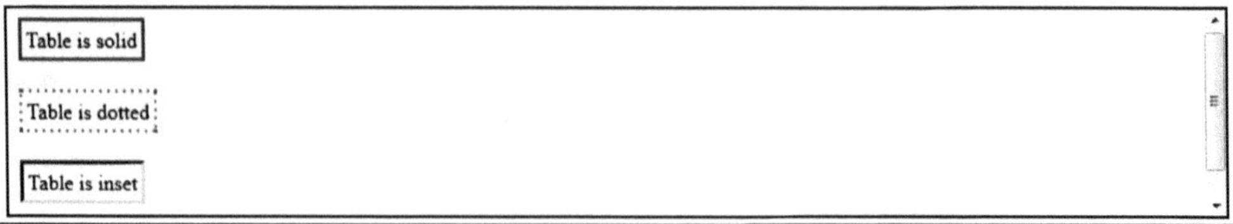

(ii) CSS border color:

- We can set the color of borders using the border-color property.

  Syntax: `border-color: value;`

  value could be color name, hexadecimal number, RGB color code or transparent

Example for CSS border color.

```
<!DOCTYPE html>
<head>
<style type="text/css">
table.first{
border-color: rgb( 100, 200, 300);
border-style: dotted;
}
table.second{
border-color: #786786;
border-style: solid;
}
p.first{
border-color: red;
border-style: outset;
}
p.second{
border-color: transparent;
border-style: dashed;
}
</style>
</head>
<body>
<p class="first">This is a paragraph</p>
<p class="second">This is a paragraph</p>
<table class="first">
<tr><td>Table 1</tr></td>
</table><br/>
<table class="second">
<tr><td>Table 2</tr></td>
</table>
</body>
</html>
```

Output:

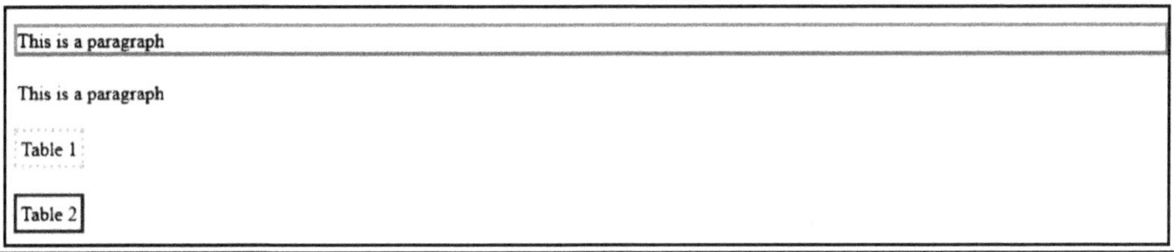

(iii) CSS border width:

- We can set the width of borders using the border-width property.

  Syntax: `border-width: value;`

  value could be medium, thin, thick or length

Example for CSS border width.

```
<!DOCTYPE html>
<head>
<style type="text/css">
p.first{
border-width: thin;
border-style: dotted;
}
p.second{
border-width: 3px;
border-style: solid;
}
</style>
</head>
<body>
<p class="first">width is thin</p>
<p class="second">width is 3px</p>
</body>
</html>
```

Output:

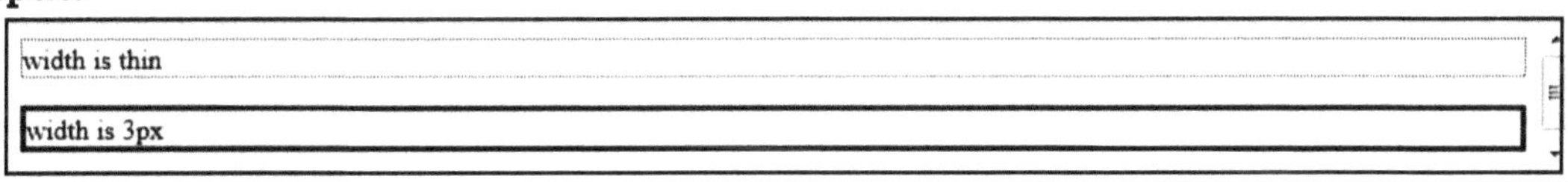

(iv) CSS border sides:

- We can position the border sides using the border-top, border-bottom, border-left and border-right properties.

Example for CSS border sides.

```
<!DOCTYPE html>
<head>
<style type="text/css">
table.first{
border-top-color: green;
border-top-style: groove;
border-top-width: 3px;
}
table.second{
border-bottom-color: green;
border-bottom-style: groove;
border-bottom-width: 3px;
}
table.third{
border-left-color: green;
border-left-style: groove;
border-left-width: 3px;
}
table.fourth{
border-right-color: green;
border-right-style: groove;
border-right-width: 3px;
}
</style>
</head>
<body>
<table class="first">
<tr><td>FIRST TABLE</td></td>
</table><br/>
<table class="second">
<tr><td>SECOND TABLE</td></td>
</table><br/>
<table class="third">
<tr><td>THIRD TABLE</td></td>
</table><br/>
<table class="fourth">
<tr><td>FOURTH TABLE</td></td>
</table>
</body>
</html>
```

Output:

5. CSS Box properties: [S-17, W-17]

- All HTML elements can be considered as boxes.
- CSS treats each element in our HTML document as a "box" with a bunch of different properties that determine where it appears on the page.
- The CSS box model is essentially a box that wraps around every HTML element.
- It is used to create the design and layout of web pages.
- It consists of: margins, borders, padding, and the actual content.
  - Explanation of the different parts:
    - Content - The content of the box, where text and images appear.
    - Padding - Clears an area around the content. The padding is transparent.
    - Border - A border that goes around the padding and content.
    - Margin - Clears an area outside the border. The margin is transparent.
- The image below illustrates the box model:

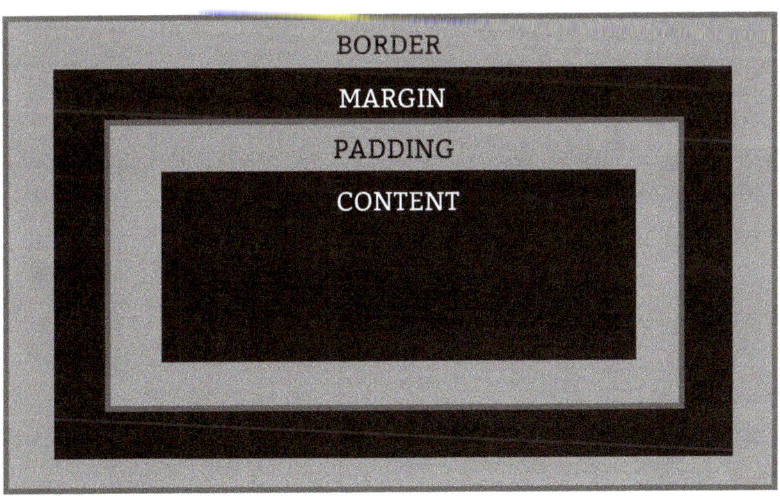

Example for CSS box.

```
<!DOCTYPE html>
<html>
<head>
<style>
div {
  background-color: lightgrey;
```

```
  width: 300px;
  border: 15px solid green;
  padding: 50px;
  margin: 20px;
}
</style>
</head>
<body>
<h2> box Model</h2>
<p>box Model.</p>
<div>Content of box Model.</div>
</body>
</html>
```

Output:

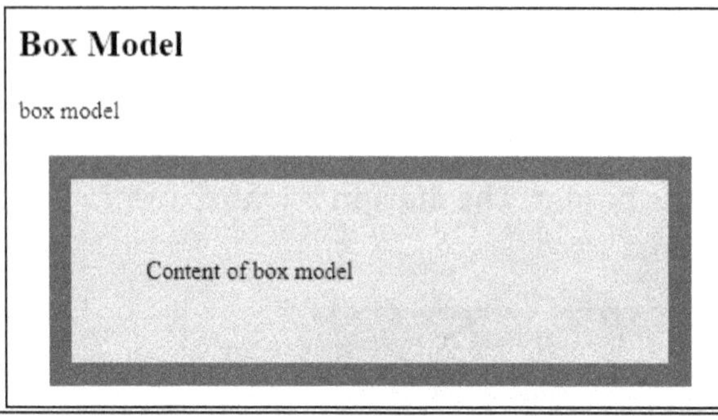

6. CSS list styles properties: [S-17]

- The appearance of ordered and unordered lists can be controlled using the list style properties.
- The list style properties are: list style type, list style image and list style position.

(i) CSS list style type:

- We can add circles, squares, romans etc. to ordered and unordered lists using the list-style-type property.

  Syntax: `list-style-type: value;`

  value could be disc, circle, square, decimal, lower-roman, upper-roman, lower-alpha or upper-alpha.

Example for CSS list style type.

```
<!DOCTYPE html>
<head>
<style type="text/css">
ol { list-style-type: square; }
ul { list-style-type: upper-alpha; }
</style>
```

```
</head>
<body>
<ol>
<li>Facebook</li>
<li>Twitter</li>
<li>Google+</li>
<li>Myspace</li>
</ol>
<ul>
<li>Facebook</li>
<li>Twitter</li>
<li>Google+</li>
<li>Myspace</li>
</ul>
</body>
</html>
```

Output:

▪ Facebook
▪ Twitter
▪ Google+
▪ Myspace

A. Facebook
B. Twitter
C. Google+
D. Myspace

(ii) CSS list style image:

- We can add images to ordered and unordered lists using the list-style-image property.

  Syntax: `list-style-image: url(image-path);`

Example for CSS list style image.

```
<!DOCTYPE html>
<head>
<style type="text/css">
ol { list-style-image:url("arrow1.gif"); }
ul { list-style-image: url("star1.jpg"); }
</style>
</head>
<body>
<ol>
<li>Facebook</li>
<li>Twitter</li>
<li>Google+</li>
```

```
<li>Myspace</li>
</ol>
<ul>
<li>Facebook</li>
<li>Twitter</li>
<li>Google+</li>
<li>Myspace</li>
</ul>
</body>
</html>
```

Output:

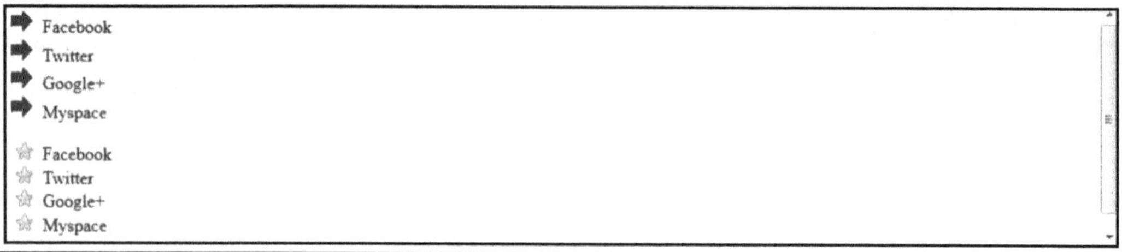

(iii) CSS list style position:

- We can control the position of ordered and unordered lists using the list-style-position property.

  Syntax: `list-style-position: value;`

  value could be inside or outside.

Example for CSS list style position.

```
<!DOCTYPE html>
<head>
<style type="text/css">
ol { list-style-position: inside; }
ul { list-style-position: outside; }
</style>
</head>
<body>
<p>This list is positioned inside</p>
<ol>
<li>Facebook</li>
<li>Twitter</li>
<li>Google+</li>
<li>Myspace</li>
</ol>
<p>This list is positioned outside</p>
```

```
<ul>
<li>Facebook</li>
<li>Twitter</li>
<li>Google+</li>
<li>Myspace</li>
</ul>
</body>
</html>
```

Output:

7. CSS Links:

- Using link properties we can set colors for visited links, unvisited links, active links etc.
- The link properties are: a:link (for unvisited links), a:visited (for visited links), a:hover (for mouseover links), a:active (changes color as the link is pressed), a:focus (for keyboard tabs).

Example for CSS links.

```
<!DOCTYPE html>
<head>
<style type="text/css">
a:link { color: green; }
a:visited { color: blue; }
a:active { color: red; }
a:hover { color: yellow; }
a:focus { color: black; }
</style>
</head>
<body>
<h1><a href="#"> Click me </a><br/></h1>
</body>
</html>
```

Output:

8. Positioning with Style Sheet:

- The position property changes how elements are positioned on our webpage.

  Syntax: `position: value;`

  Values are static, relative, absolute and fix.

(i) Static:

State positioning is by default the way an element will appear in the normal flow of our HTML file. It is not necessary to declare a position of static. Doing so, is no different than not declaring it at all.

Syntax: `position: static;`

(ii) Relative:

- Positioning an element relatively places the element in the normal flow of our HTML file and then offsets it by some amount using the properties left, right, top and bottom. This may cause the element to overlap other elements that are on the page, which of course may be the effect that is required.

  Syntax: `position: relative;`

(iii) Absolute:

Positioning an element absolutely, removes the element from the normal flow of our HTML file and positions it to the top left of it's nearest parent element that has a position declared other than static. If no parent element with a position other than static exists then it will be positioned from the top left of the browser window.

Syntax: `position: absolute;`

(iv) Fixed:

Positioning an element with the fixed value, is the same as absolute except the parent element is always the browser window. It makes no difference if the fixed element is nested inside other positioned elements.

Furthermore, an element that is positioned with a fixed value, will not scroll with the document. It will remain in its position regardless of the scroll position of the page.

Syntax: `position: fixed;`

When positioning element with relative, absolute or fixed values the following properties are used to offset the element: top, left, right and bottom.

Syntax: `position: absolute; top: 10px; right: 10px;`

9. CSS Margins:

- As we may have guessed, the margin property declares the margin between an HTML element and the elements around it.
- The margin property can be set for the top, left, right and bottom of an element, like this:

```
margin-top: length percentage or auto;
margin-left: length percentage or auto;
margin-right: length percentage or auto;
margin-bottom: length percentage or auto;
```

- As we can also see in the above example we have three choices or values for the margin property i.e. length, percentage and auto.
- We can also declare all the margins of an element in a single property as follows:

```
margin: 10px 10px 10px 10px;
```

- If we declare all four values as we have above, the order is as follows:
  1. top
  2. right
  3. bottom
  4. left
- If only one value is declared, it sets the margin on all sides.

```
margin: 10px;
```

- If we only declare two or three values, the undeclared values are taken from the opposing side.

```
margin: 10px 10px; /* 2 values */
margin: 10px 10px 10px; /* 3 values */
```

- We can set the margin property to negative values. If we do not declare the margin value of an element, the margin is 0 (zero).

```
margin: -10 px;
```

- Elements like paragraphs have default margins in some browsers, to combat this set the margin to 0 (zero).

```
p(margin; 0,)
```

- We can see in the example below, the elements for this site are set to by 20px (pixels) from the body,

```
body
{
    margin: 20 px;
    background: #eeeeee;
    font-size: small;
    font-family: Tahoma, Arial, "Trebuchet MS", Helvetica, sans-serif;
    text-align: left;
}
```

10. CSS Padding:

- Padding is the distance between the border of an HTML element and the content within it.
- Most of the rules for margins also apply to padding, except there is no "auto" value and negative values cannot be declared for padding.

```
padding-top: length percentage;
padding-left: length percentage;
padding-right: length percentage;
padding-bottom: length percentage;
```

- As we can also see in the above example we have 2 choices of values for the padding property,
  - length
  - percentage
- We can also declare all the padding of an element in a single property as follows:

```
padding: 10px 10px 10px 10px;
```

- If we declare all 4 values as we have above, the order is as follows:
  1. top
  2. right
  3. bottom
  4. left
- If only one value is declared, it sets the padding on all sides.

```
padding: 10px;
```

- If we only declare two or three values, the undeclared values are taken from the opposing side, like this.

```
padding: 10px 10px; /* 2 values */
padding: 10px 10px 10px; /* 3 values */
```

- If we do not declare the padding value of an element, the padding is 0 (zero).
- We can see in the example below, the main container for this site has 30px (pixels) of padding between the border and the text.

```
#container
{
    width: 70%;
    margin: auto;
    padding: 30 px;
    border: 1px solid #666;
    background: #ffffff;
}
{
    padding: 20px;
    border: 1px solid #666;
    background: #ffffff;
}
```

4.6 OVERVIEW AND FEATURES OF CSS2 AND CSS3

CSS2:

- Cascading Style Sheets Level 2 (CSS2) is the second version of cascading style sheets developed by W3C. It's a declarative language used to enhance the hyperextensive text markup language. CSS2 is a subset of Cascading Style Sheets Level 1 and has enhanced capabilities like:

- Media types concept.
- Aural style sheets.
- Features for internationalization.
- Extended font selection.
- Automatic numbering and generated content.
- Cursors.
- Dynamic outlines.
- Capability to control content overflow, clipping.
- Absolute, fixed and relative positioning.
- Extended selector mechanism.

- Currently, W3C does not provide any CSS2 recommendations. CSS2 have backward compatibility, so all valid CSS1 is also valid CSS2.
- Compared to CSS1, which is short and concise, CSS2 was voluminous.
- CSS2 has the following main features:
  - **Aural Style Sheets:** New style properties for defining the aural style sheet for documents.
  - **Paging:** Definition of how pages need to be displayed or printed. This made cropping, registering marks and other layout features possible.
  - **Media Types:** Different style rules for different types of media was introduced in CSS2.
  - **International Accessibility Features:** More list styles were available for international documents. This included bidirectional text support as well as language sensitive quotation marks.
  - **Font:** More fonts were defined and available for use.
  - **Positioning:** CSS2 introduced the relative, absolute positioning and the placement determination within a document. This really helped the continuous media.
  - **Cursors:** CSS2 defined the manner in which the cursor would respond to various actions.

CSS3:

- The development of style sheet was to make the markup language more impressive. It was discovered around 1980s in the beginning of the SGML.
- The third level of CSS was started to develop around 1998. And till 2009, it was under development. The first working draft of CSS3 came in 19-01-2001. And since the first introduction still it is under construction.
- There were some certain shortcomings in CSS2 and due to its unlikeness the developer introduced CSS3. It is divided into different modules according to its specifications. Though the first working draft of CSS3 came on 19-01-2001, but it was initially declared early in the June 1999.
- Cascading Style Sheets (CSS) is a style sheet language used for describing the look and formatting of a document written in a markup language.CSS3 is a latest standard of css earlier versions(CSS2).

- The main difference between CSS2 and CSS3 is follows:
  - Media Queries
  - Namespaces
  - Selectors Level 3
  - Color

Features of CSS3:

- **CSS Animations and Transitions:** There are two ways to create CSS animations. The first is very easy, it is done through animating the changes of CSS properties with the transition declaration. With transitions, we can create hover or mouse down effects, or we can trigger the animation by changing the style of an element with JavaScript. We can see the transition below by hovering over the planet - this will cause the rocket to close in.

  The second way for defining animations is a bit more complicated - it involves the description of specific moments of the animation with the code>@keyframe rule. This allows us to have repeating animations that don't depend on user actions or JavaScript to get triggered.
- **Calculating Values With calc():** Another new CSS feature is the calc() function. It allows us to do simple arithmetic calculations in CSS. We can use it anywhere a length or a size is required.
- **Advanced Selectors:** CSS3 introduced a number of powerful selectors that can make our layouts cleaner, and our style sheets more awesome.
- **Generated Content and Counters**: Generated content is a powerful tool in the hands of developers, made available by the ::before and ::after pseudo elements. This feature lets us use less HTML to achieve the same layouts. This is especially beneficial in cases where we need extra box shadows or other visual elements that would require extra spans or divs.
- **Gradients**: Gradients give web designers the power to create smooth transitions between colors without having to resort to images.
- **Webfonts:** We can use code>@font-face rule, which lets us define the name, characteristics and source files for fonts, which we can later refer in our font/font-family declarations.
- **Border Images:** The border-image property allows us to display custom designed borders around elements. The borders are contained in a single image (sprite), with each region of that image corresponding to a different part of the border.
- **Media Queries:** The media query can contain checks for the device resolution and orientation, color depth, pixel density and more. Media queries are surprisingly easy to use - all we need to do is to enclose CSS styles in a block guarded by a code>@media rule. Each code>@media block is activated when one or more conditions are met.
- **Multiple Backgrounds:** With multiple backgrounds, designers can achieve very interesting effects. They can stack different images as backgrounds of the same element. Each image (or layer) can be moved and animated independently.

Summary

- Introduction of CSS provided good level of separation on use of markup elements for structuring web page and their use for style or presentation of web page.
- Cascading Style Sheet i.e. CSS is the language which is designed with the intension to present the content for making the web pages more presentable.
- A CSS comprises of style rules that are interpreted by the browser and then applied to the corresponding elements in our document.
- A style rule is made of three parts: Selector, Property and Value.
- There are three types of style sheet: Internal, Embedded and External.
- The CSS background properties are used to define the background effects.
- We can change the text size, color, style, make it bold or light etc using CSS font properties.
- Using CSS text properties we can control the text spacing, decoration, alignment or transform the text to upper or lowercase.
- CSS border properties allow us to customize the borders.
- The appearance of ordered and unordered lists can be controlled using the list style properties.
- The position property changes how elements are positioned on our web page.
- Padding is the distance between the border of an HTML element and the content within it.
- Cascading Style Sheets Level 2 (CSS2) is the second version of cascading style sheets.
- CSS2 is a subset of Cascading Style Sheets Level 1 and has enhanced capabilities.
- There were some certain shortcomings in CSS2 and due to its unlikeness the developer introduced CSS3.

Check Your Understanding

1. If we want define style for an unique element, then which CSS selector will we use?
   (a) Id (b) text
   (c) class (d) name
2. Which of the following selector selects all elements of E that have the attribute attr that end with the given value?
   (a) E[attr^=value] (b) E[attr$=value]
   (c) E[attr*=value] (d) none of the mentioned
3. Which of the following selector selects the elements that are checked?
   (a) E ~ F (b) ::after
   (c) :checked (d) none of the mentioned
4. By applying an _______ a style can be applied to just a single tag.
   (a) class rule (b) element rule
   (c) id rule (d) none of the mentioned

5. Which of the following value is supposed to be a slightly bolder weight that standard bold in font attribute?
   (a) emphasize (b) light
   (c) lighter (d) dark
6. Which of the following value specifies whether the user agent is allowed to synthesize bold or oblique font faces when a font family lacks bold or italic faces?
   (a) font-weight (b) font-synthesis
   (c) font-kerning (d) font-variant
7. Identify the CSS property defining bottom-left corner shape of the border?
   (a) border-radius (b) border-corner-radius
   (c) border-bottom-left-radius (d) border-left-radius
8. Which of the following sets the color of any text decoration, such as underlines, overlines, and strike throughs?
   (a) text-font (b) text-format
   (c) text-color (d) text-decoration-color
9. Which of the following CSS property determines how overflowed content that is not displayed is signaled to the users?
   (a) text-flow (b) text-underflow
   (c) text-overflow (d) none of the mentioned
10. Which of the following sets the mode for the overline text decoration, determining whether the text decoration affects the space characters or not?
    (a) text-decoration (b) text-mode-overflow
    (c) text-mode (d) text-overline-mode
11. Which of the following property sets list-style-type, list-style-position, and list style-image?
    (a) style (b) list-style
    (c) menu-style (d) img-style
12. Which of the following property defines labels for a list of items?
    (a) list-shape (b) list-style
    (c) list-type (d) list-style-type

Answers

1. (a)	2. (b)	3. (c)	4. (c)	5. (d)	6. (b)	7. (c)	8. (d)	9. (c)	10. (b)
				11. (b)	12.(d)				

Practice Questions

Q.1 Answer the following Question in short.

1. What is CSS? Give its syntax.
2. State the use of CSS.
3. List three parts of style rule.
4. List types of selectors.
5. List types of style sheets.
6. State the use of background properties.
7. State the use of box properties.
8. Enlist four parts of box model.

Q.2 Answer the following Question in detail.

1. Explain CSS ID in detail.
2. Enlist various border properties of CSS.
3. Enlist various text properties of CSS.
4. Enlist various font properties of CSS.
5. Enlist various margin properties of CSS.
6. What are the types of CSS? Explain in detail.
7. Explain embedded style sheet with example.
8. What is inline stylesheet? Explain in detail.
9. Differentiate between CSS2 and CSS3.
10. What is CSS3? Enlist its features.

Previous Exams Questions

Summer 2019

1. Explain CSS with an example. **[4 M]**

Ans. Refer to Section 4.3.

2. Write HTML and CSS code to generate the following output.
(Use inline style sheet). **[4 M]**

INDIA

- Taj Mahal
- India Gate
- Bibika Makbara
- Mysore Palace

Ans. Refer to Section 4.4.1.

Summer 2018

1. List any four benefits of CSS. **[2 M]**

Ans. Refer to Section 4.2.1.

2. Explain CSS with example. **[4 M]**

Ans. Refer to Section 4.3.

Winter 2017

1. List box properties in CSS. **[2 M]**

Ans. Refer to Section 4.5.

2. What is selector and list types of selector? **[2 M]**

Ans. Refer to Section 4.3.

3. Explain types of CSS with example. **[4 M]**

Ans. Refer to Section 4.4.

Summer 2017

1. List box properties in CSS. **[2 M]**

Ans. Refer to Section 4.5.

2. Explain types of CSS with example. **[4 M]**

Ans. Refer to Section 4.4.

Summer 2016

1. Give any two text formatting tags. **[2 M]**

Ans. Refer to Section 4.5.

2. Give any two properties of Border. **[2 M]**

Ans. Refer to Section 4.5.

3. Explain CSS in detail. **[4 M]**

Ans. Refer to Section 4.2.1.

■■■

5... JavaScript

Objectives...

- To understand Identifier, operator, control structure, functions.
- To study Document Object Model.
- To learn DOM Objects.
- To study predefined functions, math and string functions.
- To study Array in JavaScript.
- To learn Event handling in JavaScript.

5.1 INTRODUCTION

- JavaScript is the most popular scripting language on the Internet and works in all major browsers, such as Internet Explorer, Firefox, Chrome, Opera and Safari.
- JavaScript usually runs on the client-side (the browser's side), as opposed to server-side (on the web server). One benefit of doing this is performance. On the client side, JavaScript is loaded into the browser and can run as soon as it is called. Without running on the client-side, the page would need to refresh each time we needed a script to run.
- JavaScript was written for the express purpose of adding interactivity to web pages.
- JavaScript is a scripting language designed primarily for adding interactivity to web pages and creating web applications.
- A scripting language is a light weight programming language.
- Scripting languages are of two types:
  1. Client-side scripting languages, and
  2. Server-side scripting languages.
- Client-server script runs at user's end i.e. the browser executes the scripts. JavaScript is an example of a client side script that is interpreted by the client browser.
- Where as server-side scripting language is executed on a web server. PHP is a server side script that is interpreted on the server.

<script> Tag:

- One of the most usual ways we will use JavaScript is to display text, as if we were using HTML. Indeed, added just a few instructions, we can use any of the HTML tags and make them part of our script.

- To set the instructions of a script, the section that has the script must start with the <script> tag and end with the </script> tag, as follows:

  Syntax: `<script>...........</script>`
- Because a script is written in a particular language that is not HTML and because there are various scripting languages, to use a script, we should let the browser know what scripting language we are using.
- To let the browser know, type the word Language, followed by the = sign, followed by the name of the script language included in double-quotes. For example, to use JavaScript in a page, start the section with

```
<script language="JavaScript">
```

  and end it with the closing tag. Therefore the scripting section can be delimited with:

```
<script Language="JavaScript>
</script>
```

5.1.1 Features of JavaScript

- Various features of JavaScript are listed below:
  1. JavaScript is a object-based scripting language.
  2. It is light weighted.
  3. JavaScript is a scripting language and it is not java.
  4. JavaScript is interpreter based scripting language.
  5. JavaScript is case sensitive.
  6. JavaScript is object based language as it provides predefined objects.
  7. Every statement in JavaScript must be terminated with semicolon (;).

5.1.2 Embedding JavaScript

- The HTML<script> tag is used to insert a JavaScript into an HTML page.
- Browser will not know where javascript has started. So, in order to tell it where javascript has started we use a special HTML tag, <script>.

  Syntax of JavaScript:

```
<script type="text/javascript">
javascript comes here .........
</script>
```

- <script> and </script> informs browser that everything in between is a scripting language. The attribute type, is given a value "text/javascript", specifying that the scripting language is JavaScript.
- JavaScript can be added in the <body> or in the <head> sections of an HTML code.

Example of embedding JavaScript in <head> tag:

```
<html>
<head>
<title>Javascript Example </title>
<script type="text/javascript">
```

```
document.write("My first Javascript");
</script>
</head>
</html>
```

Output:

```
My first Javascript
```

Example shows embedded javascript in <body > tag.

```
<html>
<body>
<script type="text/javascript">
document.write("Hello World!");
</script>
</body>
</html>
```

Output:

```
Hello World!
```

- Document is the part of browser where we see webpage content, document.write will write the text in parentheses (round brackets) to the browser document. In our case, the text "My First Javascript" will be written. The double quotes are important when we want to print/write the text in it. And every statement in javascript ends with a semicolon(;).

Embedding a JavaScript using external file:

```
<!DOCTYPE html>
<html>
<body>
<h1>My Web Page</h1>
<p id="demo">A Paragraph.</p>
<button type="button" onclick="myFunction()">Nirali Prakashan</button>
<p><strong>Note:</strong> The actual script is in an external script file
called "myScript.js".</p>
<script type="text/javascript" src="myScript.js"></script>
</body>
</html>
```

5.1.3 Advantages and Disadvantages of JavaScript

Advantages of JavaScript:

1. **Less Server Interaction:** We can validate user input before sending the page off to the server. This saves server traffic, which means less load on our server.
2. **Immediate Feedback to the Visitors:** They do not have to wait for a page reload to see if they have forgotten to enter something.

3. **Increased Interactivity:** We can create interfaces that react when the user hovers over them with a mouse or activates them via the keyboard.
4. **Richer Interfaces:** We can use JavaScript to include such items as drag-and-drop components and sliders to give a Rich Interface to our site visitors.
5. **Speed:** Being client-side, JavaScript is very fast because any code functions can be run immediately instead of having to contact the server and wait for an answer.
6. **Simplicity:** JavaScript is relatively simple to learn and implement.
7. **Versatility:** JavaScript plays nicely with other languages and can be used in a huge variety of applications.
8. **Server Load:** Being client-side reduces the demand on the website server.

Limitations with JavaScript:

1. Client-side JavaScript does not allows the reading or writing of files. This has been kept for security reason.
2. JavaScript can not be used for Networking applications because there is no such support available.
3. JavaScript does not have any multithreading or multiprocess capabilities.
4. **Security:** Because the code executes on the users computer, in some cases it can be exploited for malicious purposes. This is one reason some people choose to disable JavaScript.
5. **Reliance on End User:** JavaScript is sometimes interpreted differently by different browsers. Whereas server-side scripts will always produce the same output, client-side scripts can be a little unpredictable. Don't be overly concerned by this though - as long as we test our script in all the major browsers we should be safe.

5.2 IDENTIFIER

- An identifier is a symbol that represents, names a piece of data.
- An identifier can represent a function or a variable.
- JavaScript identifiers are used to name the JavaScript language entities like variable, object, function and to provide labels for certain loops in JavaScript code.
- JavaScript identifiers must start with character followed by subsequent characters can be letter, a digit, an underscore; Dollar sign ($) also allow.
- With some versions of JavaScript, dollar signs are not legal in identifiers. The best practice of defining JavaScript identifiers is to avoid the use of dollar signs.
- We cannot use JavaScript reserved keywords as a JavaScript identifiers like:

```
var intNum = 82                    //intNum is JavaScript Identifiers
var PI = 3.14                      //PI is JavaScript Identifiers
var strInfo="This is a string"     // strInfo is JavaScript Identifiers
var strGreet='Hello!';             //strGreet is JavaScript Identifiers
var arrAnimal={"cat","dog")        //arrAnimal in JavaScript Identifiers
```

5.3 OPERATORS

- An operator is used to transform one or more values into a single resultant values and the values to which the operator is applied is referred as operands.
- JavaScript operators are used to perform an operation. There are different types of operators for different uses.
- Simple example, answer can be given using expression 4 + 5 is equal to 9. Here 4 and 5 are called operands and + is called operator.
- JavaScript language supports following type of operators.
  1. Arithmetic operators.
  2. Comparison operators.
  3. Logical (or Relational) operators.
  4. Assignment operators.
  5. Conditional (or ternary) operators.

1. Arithmetic Operators:

- Arithmetic operators are used to perform arithmetic between variables and/or values.
- The standard arithmetic operators in JavaScript are addition (+), subtraction (–), multiplication (*), division (/) and modulus (%). These operators work as in standard algebra.
- Following table shows arithmetic operators supported by JavaScript language. Assume variable A holds 10 and variable B holds 20 then:

Operator	Description	Example
+ (Addition operator)	Adds two operands.	A + B = 30
– (Subtraction operator)	Subtracts second operand from the first.	A – B = –10
* (Multiplication operator)	Multiply both operands.	A * B = 200
/ (Division operator)	Divide numerator by denumerator.	B / A = 2
% (Modulus operator)	Modulus operator and remainder of after an integer division.	B % A = 0
++ (Increment operator)	Increases integer value by one.	A++ = 11
-- (Decrement operator)	Decreases integer value by one.	A-- = 9

Example for Arithmetic Operators.

```
<!DOCTYPE html>
<head>
<title> Arithmetic Operators Example</title>
<script type="text/javascript">
var x = 16;
var y = 5;
```

```
var sum = x + y;
var sub = x - y;
var mul = x * y;
var div = x / y;
var mod = x % y;
document.write("addition is "+sum+"<br>");
document.write("subtraction is "+sub+"<br>");
document.write("multiplication is "+mul+"<br>");
document.write("division is "+div+"<br>");
document.write("remainder is "+mod+"<br>");
</script>
</head>
</html>
```

Output:

```
addition is 21
subtraction is 11
multiplication is 80
division is 3.2
remainder is 1
```

2. Comparison Operators:

- Comparison operators are used in logical statements to determine equality or difference between variables or values.
- Comparison operators are used to compare a condition and are always inside conditional statements. A comparison evaluate to their true or false. This true and false values are called Booleans.
- Following table shows comparison operators supported by JavaScript and assume variable A holds 10 and B holds 20.

Operator	Sign	Description
Equal	==	If both operands are equal, returns true.
Identical equal	===	If both operands are equal and/or same data type, returns true.
Not equal	!=	If both operands are not equal, returns true.
Identical not equal	!==	If both operands are not equal and/or same data type, returns true.
Greater than	>	If left operand larger than right operand, return true.
Less then	<	If left operand smaller than right operand, return true.
Greater than, equal	>=	If left operand larger or equal than right operand, return true.
Less than, equal	<=	If left operand smaller or equal than right operand, return true.

Example for Comparison Operators.

```
<!DOCTYPE html>
<body>
<script type="text/javascript">
var a = 20;
var b = 30;
var linebreak = "<br />";
document.write("(a == b) => ");
result = (a == b);
document.write(result);
document.write(linebreak);
document.write("(a < b) => ");
result = (a < b);
document.write(result);
document.write(linebreak);
document.write("(a > b) => ");
result = (a > b);
document.write(result);
document.write(linebreak);
document.write("(a != b) => ");
result = (a != b);
document.write(result);
document.write(linebreak);
document.write("(a >= b) => ");
result = (a >= b);
document.write(result);
document.write(linebreak);
document.write("(a <= b) => ");
result = (a <= b);
document.write(result);
document.write(linebreak);
</script>
<p>Set the variables to different values and different operators and then
try...</p>
</body>
</html>
```

Output:

```
(a == b) => false
(a < b) => true
(a > b) => false
(a != b) => true
(a >= b) => false
(a <= b) => true
Set the variables to different values and different operators and then
try...
```

3. Logical Operators:

- Logical operators are used to determine the logic between variables or values.
- Using logical operators, we can test two or more conditions in one line code.
- There are following logical operators supported by JavaScript and assume variable A holds 10 and variable B holds 20 then:

Operator	Description	Example
&& (Logical AND Operator)	If both the operands are non zero then then condition becomes true.	(A && B) is true.
|| (Logical OR Operator)	If any of the two operands are non zero then then condition becomes true.	(A || B) is true.
! (Logical NOT Operator)	Use to reverses the logical state of its operand. If a condition is true then Logical NOT operator will make false.	!(A && B) is false.

Example for Logical Operators:

```
<!DOCTYPE html>
<body>
<script type="text/javascript">
var a = true;
var b = false;
var linebreak = "<br />";
document.write("(a &&  b) => ");
result = (a && b);
document.write(result);
document.write(linebreak);
document.write("(a || b) => ");
result = (a || b);
document.write(result);
document.write(linebreak);
```

```
document.write("!(a && b) => ");
result = (!(a && b));
document.write(result);
document.write(linebreak);
</script>
<p>Set the variables to different values and different operators and then
try...</p>
</body>
</html>
```

Output:

```
(a && b) => false
(a || b) => true
!(a && b) => true
Set the variables to different values and different operators and then try...
```

4. Bitwise Operators:

- Bitwise operators act upon the individual bits of their operands.
- Following table gives bitwise operators supported by JavaScript and assume variable A holds 2 and variable B holds 3 then:

Operator	Sign	Description
Bitwise AND	&	Return bitwise AND operation for given two operands.
Bitwise OR	|	Return bitwise OR operation for given two operands.
Bitwise XOR	^	Return bitwise XOR operation for given two operands.
Bitwise NOT	~	Return bitwise NOT operation for given operand.
Bitwise Shift Left	<<	Return left shift of given operands.
Bitwise Shift Right	>>	Return right shift of given operands.
Bitwise Unsigned Shift Right	>>>	Return right shift without consider sign of given operands.

Example of Bitwise Operators.

```
<html>
<body>
<script type="text/javascript">
var a = 3;  // Bit presentation 11
var b = 4;  // Bit presentation 12
```

```
var linebreak = "<br />";
document.write("(a &  b) => ");
result = (a & b);
document.write(result);
document.write(linebreak);
document.write("(a | b) => ");
result = (a | b);
document.write(result);
document.write(linebreak);
document.write("(a ^ b) => ");
result = (a ^ b);
document.write(result);
document.write(linebreak);
document.write("(~b) => ");
result = (~b);
document.write(result);
document.write(linebreak);
document.write("(a << b) => ");
result = (a << b);
document.write(result);
document.write(linebreak);
document.write("(a >> b) => ");
result = (a >> b);
document.write(result);
document.write(linebreak);
</script>
<p>Set the variables to different values and different operators and then
try...</p>
</body>
</html>
```

Output:

```
(a & b) => 0
(a | b) => 7
(a ^ b) => 7
(~b) => -5
(a << b) => 48
(a >> b) => 0
Set the variables to different values and different operators and then
try...
```

5. Assignment Operators:

- Assignment operators are used to assign values to JavaScript variables.
- There are following assignment operators supported by JavaScript.

Operator	Description	Example
= (Simple assignment operator)	Assigns values from right side operands to left side operand.	C = A + B will assignee value of A + B into C
+= (Add AND assignment operator)	It adds right operand to the left operand and assign the result to left operand.	C += A is equivalent to C = C + A
-= (Subtract AND assignment operator)	It subtracts right operand from the left operand and assign the result to left operand.	C -= A is equivalent to C = C - A
*= (Multiply AND assignment operator)	It multiplies right operand with the left operand and assign the result to left operand.	C *= A is equivalent to C = C * A
/= (Divide AND assignment operator)	It divides left operand with the right operand and assign the result to left operand.	C /= A is equivalent to C = C / A
%= (Modulus AND assignment operator)	It takes modulus using two operands and assign the result to left operand.	C %= A is equivalent to C = C % A

Example for Assignment Operator.

```
<html>
<body>
<script type="text/javascript">
var a = 44;
var b = 10;
var linebreak = "<br />";
document.write("Value of a => (a = b) => ");
result = (a = b);
```

```
document.write(result);
document.write(linebreak);
document.write("Value of a => (a += b) => ");
result = (a += b);
document.write(result);
document.write(linebreak);
document.write("Value of a => (a -= b) => ");
result = (a -= b);
document.write(result);
document.write(linebreak);
document.write("Value of a => (a *=  b) => ");
result = (a *= b);
document.write(result);
document.write(linebreak);
document.write("Value of a => (a /= b) => ");
result = (a /= b);
document.write(result);
document.write(linebreak);
document.write("Value of a => (a %= b) => ");
result = (a %= b);
document.write(result);
document.write(linebreak);
</script>
<p>Set the variables to different values and different operators and then
try...</p>
</body>
</html>
```

Output:

```
Value of a => (a = b) => 10
Value of a => (a += b) => 20
Value of a => (a -= b) => 10
Value of a => (a *= b) => 100
Value of a => (a /= b) => 10
Value of a => (a %= b) => 0
Set the variables to different values and different operators and then
try...
```

6. Conditional Operators (?:):

- There is an operator called conditional operator. This first evaluates an expression for a true or false value and then execute one of the two given statements depending upon the result of the evaluation.
- The conditional operator has following syntax:

Operator	Description	Example
?:	Conditional Expression	If Condition is true? Then value X: Otherwise value Y.

Example for Conditional Operator.

```
<html>
<body>
<script type="text/javascript">
var a = 10;
var b = 20;
var linebreak = "<br />";
document.write("((a > b) ? 100: 200) => ");
result = (a > b) ? 100: 200;
document.write(result);
document.write(linebreak);
document.write("((a < b) ? 100: 200) => ");
result = (a < b) ? 100: 200;
document.write(result);
document.write(linebreak);
</script>
<p>Set the variables to different values and different operators and then
try...</p>
</body>
</html>
```

Output:

```
((a > b) ? 100: 200) => 200
((a < b) ? 100: 200) => 100
Set the variables to different values and different operators and then
try...
```

7. typeof Operator:

- The typeof is a unary operator that is placed before its single operand, which can be of any type. Its value is a string indicating the data type of the operand.
- The typeof operator evaluates to "number", "string", or "boolean" if its operand is a number, string, or boolean value and returns true or false based on the evaluation.

- Here, is the list of return values for the typeof Operator:

Type	String Returned by typeof
Number	"number"
String	"string"
Boolean	"boolean"
Object	"object"
Function	"function"
Undefined	"undefined"
Null	"object"

Example for typeof operator.

```
<!DOCTYPE html>
<body>
<script type="text/javascript">
var a = 10;
var b = "String";
var linebreak = "<br />";
result = (typeof b == "string" ? "B is String": "B is Numeric");
document.write("Result => ");
document.write(result);
document.write(linebreak);
result = (typeof a == "string" ? "A is String": "A is Numeric");
document.write("Result => ");
document.write(result);
document.write(linebreak);
</script>
<p>Set the variables to different values and different operators and then
try...</p>
</body>
</html>
```

Output:

```
Result => B is String
Result => A is Numeric
Set the variables to different values and different operators and then
try...
```

5.4 CONTROL AND LOOPING STRUCTURE

- While writing a program, there may be a situation when we need to adopt one path out of the given two paths. So we need to make use of conditional statements that allow our program to make correct decisions and perform right actions.
- JavaScript supports conditional statements which are used to perform different actions based on different conditions.
- Very often when we write code, we want to perform different actions for different decisions. We can use conditional statements in our code to do this.
- Examples of some daily life decisions are:
  1. If it's a weekend, do not get up early.
  2. If trailer is good, watch the movie, else do not.

5.4.1 Conditional Statements

- In JavaScript we have the following conditional statements:
  1. **if Statement:** Use this statement to execute some code only if a specified condition is true.
  2. **if...else Statement:** Use this statement to execute some code if the condition is true and another code if the condition is false.
  3. **if...elseif....else Statement:** Use this statement to select one of many blocks of code to be executed.
  4. **switch Statement:** Use this statement to select one of many blocks of code to be executed.

5.4.1.1 if Statement

- The if statement is the fundamental control statement that allows JavaScript to make decisions and execute statements conditionally.
- We can use the if statement to execute some code only if a specified condition is true.

Syntax:

```
if(condition)
{
execute this statement;
}
```

- In the above syntax the keyword if specifies that what is a decision control instruction followed.
- The condition to be checked is always enclosed in round brackets (). The statements to be executed, if the condition is true, are added in curly brackets {}, normally called an if block.

Example to check whether number is equal or not.

```
<!DOCTYPE html>
<head><title>If statement</title></head>
<body>
```

```
<script type="text/javascript">
var x = 7;
var y = 7;
if(x==y)
{
document.write("Both are equal");
}
</script>
</body>
</html>
```

Output:

```
Both are equal
```

5.4.1.2 if...else Statement

- The if...else statement is the next form of control statement that allows JavaScript to execute statements in more controlled way.
- We can use the if....else statement to execute some code if a condition is true and another code if the condition is not true.
- The keyword if executes a statement only if the condition is true. It does not do anything if the condition is false.

  Syntax:

  ```
  if(condition)
  {
  execute this statement;
  }
  else
  {
  execute this statement;
  }
  ```

- In above syntax, if the condition is true, the statement in the if block is executed, and the statement in 'else' block is skipped. If the condition is false, the statement in else block is executed, and the statement in if block is skipped.

Example to check whether given number is even or odd.

```
<script>
var a=40;
if(a%2==0)
{
document.write("a is even number");
}
else{
document.write("a is odd number");
}
</script>
```

Output:

```
a is even number
```

5.4.1.3 if...else if...else Statement

- We use the if....else if...else statement to select one of several blocks of code to be executed.
- The if...else if... statement is the one level advance form of control statement that allows JavaScript to make correct decision out of several conditions.

Syntax:

```
if(condition)
{
   execute this statement;
}
else if(condition)
{
   execute this statement;
}
else
{
   execute this statement;
}
```

Example to perform if...else if...else statement.

```
<!DOCTYPE html>
<body>
<script type="text/javascript">
var your_age = 14;
var friends_age = 16;
if(your_age >= 18)
{
document.write("Get a drivers license");
}
else if(friends_age >= 18) {
document.write("Let our friend drive the car");
}
else {
document.write("Kids, stick to bicycle");
}
</script>
</body>
</html>
```

Output:

Kids, stick to bicycle

5.4.1.4 switch Statement

- Switch statement is used to execute one of the statements from many blocks of statements.
- Use the switch statement to select one of many blocks of code to be executed.
- Switch statement is like enhanced if-else if-else statement, only less confusing and more easy and simple to use.

Syntax:

```
switch(value/expression)
{
case "value1":
execute this statement1;
break;
case "value2":
execute this statement2;
break;
---
---
---
default:
executes this statement;
}
```

- The switch statement begin with keyword "switch", and round brackets that contain an expression or value.
- This expression/value is matched against the value following each "case" (in our case, value is matched against value1/value2 and so on) and if there is a match, it executes the code contained inside that case.
- The break statement indicates the end of that particular case. If we omit break, it will continue executing the statements in each of the following cases. If no match is found, it executes the default statement.
- The switch statement is used in JavaScript to execute one code from multiple expressions.

Example to write JavaScript program to display today's day using switch case.

```
<!DOCTYPE html>
<body>
<p>Click the button to display what day it is today.</p>
<button onclick="myFunction()">Click it</button>
<p id="demofor Day"></p>
<script>
function myFunction()
{
var x;
var d=new Date().getDay();
```

```
switch (d)
  {
  case 0:
    x="Today it's Sunday";
    break;
  case 1:
    x="Today it's Monday";
    break;
  case 2:
    x="Today it's Tuesday";
    break;
  case 3:
    x="Today it's Wednesday";
    break;
  case 4:
    x="Today it's Thursday";
    break;
  case 5:
    x="Today it's Friday";
    break;
  case 6:
    x="Today it's Saturday";
    break;
  }
document.getElementById("demoforDays").innerHTML=x;
}
</script>
</body>
</html>
```

default Keyword:

- We use the default keyword to specify what to do if there is no match.

Example for switch case using default keyword.

```
<!DOCTYPE html>
<body>
<p>Click the button to display a message based on what day it is
today.</p>
<button onclick="myFunction()">Click it</button>
<p id="demo1"></p>
<script>
```

```
function myFunction()
{
var x;
var d=new Date().getDay();
switch (d)
  {
  case 6:
    x="Today it's Saturday";
    break;
  case 0:
    x="Today it's Sunday";
    break;
  default:
    x="Looking forward to the Weekend";
  }
document.getElementById("demo1").innerHTML=x;
}
</script>
</body>
</html>
```

5.4.1.5 break Statement

- break statement indicates the end of that particular case.
- break statement was used to "jump out" of a switch() statement.
- The break statement can also be used to jump out of a loop.
- The break statement breaks the loop and continues executing the code after the loop (if any).

  Syntax: `break;`

Example to perform break statement.

```
<!DOCTYPE html>
<body>
<p>Click the button to do a loop with a break.</p>
<button onclick="myFunction()">Click it</button>
<p id="demo"></p>
<script>
function myFunction()
{
var x="",i=0;
for (i=0;i<10;i++)
  {
```

```
    if (i==3)
      {
      break;
      }
    x=x + "The number is " + i + "<br>";
    }
document.getElementById("demo").innerHTML=x;
}
</script>
</body>
</html>
```

5.4.1.6 continue Statement

- The continue statement breaks one iteration (in the loop), if a specified condition occurs, and continues with the next iteration in the loop.

  Syntax: `continue;`

Example to perform continue statement.

```
<!DOCTYPE html>
<body>
<p>Click the button to do a loop which will skip the step where i=3.</p>
<button onclick="myFunction()">Try it</button>
<p id="demo"></p>
<script>
function myFunction()
{
var x="",i=0;
for (i=0;i<10;i++)
  {
  if (i==3)
    {
    continue;
    }
  x=x + "The number is " + i + "<br>";
  }
document.getElementById("demo").innerHTML=x;
}
</script>
</body>
</html>
```

Labels:

- JavaScript statements can be labeled. To label JavaScript statements we proceed the statements with a colon(:).

```
label:
statements
```

- The break and the continue statements are the only JavaScript statements that can "jump out of" a code block.

  Syntax:

```
break labelname;
continue labelname;
```

- The continue statement (with or without a label reference) can only be used inside a loop.
- The break statement, without a label reference, can only be used inside a loop or a switch.
- With a label reference, it can be used to "jump out of" any JavaScript code block.

Example for labels.

```
<!DOCTYPE html>
<body>
<script>
cars=["Ritz","Alto","Bravo","Ford"];
list:
{
document.write(cars[0] + "<br>");
document.write(cars[1] + "<br>");
document.write(cars[2] + "<br>");
break list;
document.write(cars[3] + "<br>");
document.write(cars[4] + "<br>");
document.write(cars[5] + "<br>");
}
</script>
</body>
</html>
```

5.4.2 Loops

- It is often the case that we want to do something fixed number of times or until a particular condition has been met. In javascript, this repetitive operation is done using loops.
- Loops can execute a block of code a number of times.
- Loops are handy, if we want to run the same code over and over again, each time with a different value.

- JavaScript supports following kinds of loops:
  1. **for:** Loops through a block of code a number of times.
  2. **for/in:** Loops through the properties of an object.
  3. **while:** Loops through a block of code while a specified condition is true.
  4. **do/while:** Loops through a block of code while a specified condition is true.

5.4.2.1 for Loop

- The for loop is often the tool we will use when we want to create a loop.
- The for loop is the most compact form of looping and includes the following three important parts:
  1. The loop initialization where we initialize our counter to a starting value. The initialization statement is executed before the loop begins.
  2. The test statement which will test if the given condition is true or not. If condition is true then code given inside the loop will be executed otherwise loop will come out.
  3. The iteration statement where we can increase or decrease our counter.
- We can put all the three parts in a single line separated by a semicolon.

Syntax:

```
for(initialize; condition; increment)
{
execute statements;
}
```

Example to write program to print numbers between 6 to 10.

```
<!DOCTYPE html>
<head>
<script type="text/javascript">
for(var x=6; x<=10; x++)
{
document.write("The number is: " +x);
document.write("<br/>");
}
</script>
</head>
</html>
```

Output:

```
The number is: 6
The number is: 7
The number is: 8
The number is: 9
The number is: 10
```

- In above program, when the for loop is executed for the first time, the value of x is 6. Now the condition x<=10 is checked. Since x is 6, the condition is true and the statements inside the for loop gets executed.
- When control reaches the closing brackets of for loop, the control goes back to the beginning of for loop. There the value of x gets incremented by 1. Now the value of x is 7.
- Again the condition is checked and the whole process is continued until the condition is false.

5.4.2.2 for/in Loop

- There is one more loop supported by JavaScript and it is called for/in loop.
- for/in loop is used to loop through an object's properties.
- In other words the JavaScript for/in statement loops through the properties of an object.

  Syntax:

```
for (variablename in object){
    statement or block to execute
}
```

- In each iteration, one property from object is assigned to variablename and this loop continues till all the properties of the object are exhausted.

Example to perform for/in loop.

```
<!DOCTYPE html>
<body>
<p>Click the button to loop through the properties of an object named "person".</p>
<button onclick="myFunction()">Click it</button>
<p id="demo"></p>
<script>
function myFunction()
{
var x;
var txt="";
var person={fname:"Nirali",lname:"Prakashan",age:25};
for (x in person)
{
txt=txt + person[x];
}
document.getElementById("demo").innerHTML=txt;
}
</script>
</body>
</html>
```

5.4.2.3 while Loop

- The purpose of a while loop is to execute a statement or code block repeatedly as long as expression is true. Once expression becomes false, the loop will be exited.
- The while loop loops through a block of code as long as a specified condition is true.
- The keyword while creates a loop that tests an expression, and if it is true, executes a block of statements. And the loop repeats, as long as the specified condition is true.

Syntax:

```
initialize;
while (condition)
{
execute statement;
increment;
}
```

Example to write a program to display number from 3 to 10.

```
<!DOCTYPE html>
<head>
<script type="text/javascript">
var number = 3;
while (number <= 10)
{
document.write("The number is: " +number);
document.write("<br/>");
number++;
}
</script>
</head>
</html>
```

Output:

```
The number is: 3
The number is: 4
The number is: 5
The number is: 6
The number is: 7
The number is: 8
The number is: 9
The number is: 10
```

- In the statement: var number = 3, we are assigning a value 3 to a variable "number".
- In the statement: while(number <=10), we are testing a condition, i.e. testing if 3 <= 10. This condition is true, hence the while loop gets executed.
- Since, 3 <= 10, the document.write() statements gets executed. The second document.write() statement is just for a line break.

- Remember at this point the number is holding value 3. When the statement number++ is executed, it holds value 4.
- Now the condition 4 <= 10 will be checked. Since 4 <= 10, the document.write() statements are executed. After that number increments to 5. This happens until the condition (num<=10) is false.

5.4.2.4 do-while Loop

- Sometimes, we want some statements to be executed atleast once even if the condition is false for the first time. To do this we use a do-while loop.
- The do-while loop is a variant of the while loop.
- This loop will execute the code block once, before checking if the condition is true, then it will repeat the loop as long as the condition is true.
- The do-while loop is similar to the while loop except that the condition check happens at the end of the loop. This means that the loop will always be executed at least once, even if the condition is false.

Syntax:

```
do{
   Statements to be executed;
} while (expression);
```

Example for do/while loop:

```
<!DOCTYPE html>
<body>
<p>Click the button to loop through a block of as long as <em>i</em>
is less than 5.</p>
<button onclick="myFunction()">Click it</button>
<p id="demo5"></p>
<script>
function myFunction()
{
var x="",i=0;
do
  {
  x=x + "The number is " + i + "<br>";
  i++;
  }
while (i<5)
document.getElementById("demo5").innerHTML=x;
}
</script>
</body>
</html>
```

5.5 FUNCTIONS

- Like any other advance programming language, JavaScript also supports all the features necessary to write modular code using functions.
- A function is a block of code that will be executed when "someone" calls it.
- Function is a block of statements that performs certain task.
- Functions are building blocks of any programming language.
- Functions are of two types pre-defined/built-in functions and user-defined functions.
- Built-in functions are the functions that are already defined in the JavaScript. Examples are write(), alert(), prompt() etc.
- User-defined functions are defined by a user. Sometimes, this functions are simple, and sometimes they are quite complex.

Function Definition:

- Before we use a function we need to define that function.
- The most common way to define a function in JavaScript is by using the function keyword, followed by a unique function name, a list of parameters (that might be empty), and a statement block surrounded by curly braces.

  Syntax:

```
<script type="text/javascript">
function function_name(parameter-list)
{
  statements ...
}
</script>
```

- A simple function that takes no parameters called sayHelloJavaScript is defined here:

```
<script type="text/JavaScript">
function sayHelloJavaScript()
{
   alert("Hello JavaScript");
}
</script>
```

Calling a Function:

- Calling a function is using the defined function. A function can be called from any section of our code.

  Syntax: `functionName();`

  Syntax is simple, just functionName with empty brackets and a semi-colon.

Example for function in JavaScript.

```
<!DOCTYPE html>
<head>
<title>Javascript Function Example </title>
</head>
<body>
<script type="text/javascript">
function test()
{  //defining function
var a = 40;
document.write(a);
}
test();                //calling function
</script>
</body>
</html>
```

Output:

```
40
```

- We have defined a function test using keyword function. In the function block we have assigned a value 40 to variable a. The next line is document.write() statement.
- This function test() will not print 40 to the screen all by itself. It has to be called, which we are doing using the statement test();

Function Parameters:

- In the previous point, we defined a function test() without any values in the round brackets.
- In practical situations, we might need to add some values (parameters) in the round brackets.

Syntax:

```
function functionName(para_1, para_2...para_n)
{
statements to be executed;
}
```

Example for function parameter.

```
<!DOCTYPE html>
<head>
<title>Javascript Function Parameters</title>
</head>
<body>
<script type="text/javascript">
function add(x,y)
{
result = x+y;
document.write("addition is: "+result);
document.write("<br/>");
}
```

```
add(10,10);
add(23,12);
</script>
</body>
</html>
```

Output:

```
addition is: 20
addition is: 35
```

- Notice how we are passing parameter values to the function. The function add() is called twice.
- Everytime we want to add two numbers, we need not write the code for it every single time. We can write the code once, and call it as many times as we want.

return statement:

- Sometimes, we want the functions to perform some calculations and return the result, so that we can use that result outside the function. We use return statement to return a value.
- A JavaScript function can have an optional return statement. This is required if we want to return a value from a function. This statement should be the last statement in a function.
- For example, we can pass two numbers in a function and then we can expect from the function to return their multiplication in our calling program.

  Syntax: `return value;`

Example for return statement in JavaScript.

```
<!DOCTYPE html>
<head>
<title>Javascript Return statement</title>
</head>
<body>
<script type="text/javascript">
function areaRect(L,B)
{
var area = L*B;
return area;
}
x=areaRect(6,8);
document.write(x);
</script>
</body>
</html>
```

Output:

```
48
```

- areaRect(6,8); calls the function and passes values 6 and 8.
- The function calculates the area, and returns it (in our case, 48).
- Now, after the function has returned a value, areaRect(6,8) is 48. This value 48, is assigned to x.
- The statement document.write(x) will print 48 in the webpage.

5.6 DOCUMENT OBJECT MODEL (DOM) [W-16, 17, S-17, 18]

- The **Document Object Model (DOM)** is the data representation of the objects that comprise the structure and content of a document on the web.
- The DOM is a W3C (World Wide Web Consortium) standard.
- The DOM defines a standard for accessing documents:

  "The W3C Document Object Model (DOM) is a platform and language-neutral interface that permits programs and scripts to dynamically access and update the content, structure, and style of a document."

- Every web page resides inside a browser window which can be considered as an object.
- A Document object represents the HTML document that is displayed in that window.
- The Document object has various properties that refer to other objects which allow access to and modification of document content.
- The way that document content is accessed and modified is called the Document Object Model, or DOM.
- The Objects are organized in a hierarchy as shown in Fig. 5.1.

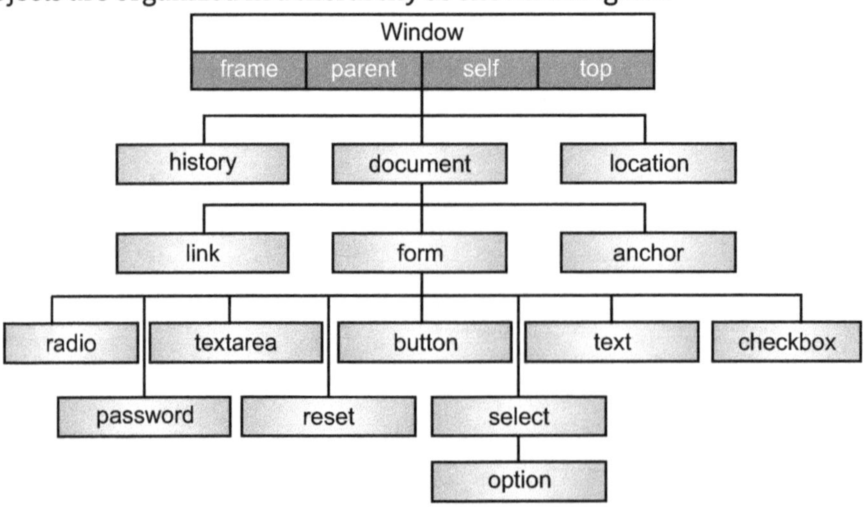

Fig. 5.1: Hierarchical structure of objects

DOM Properties:

DOM Property	Description
innerHTML	Holds the HTML inside a set of HTML tags.
nodeName	The name of an HTML element or element's attribute.
id	The "id" attribute of an HTML element.
parentNode	A reference to the node one level up in the DOM.
childNodes	An array of references to the nodes one level down in the DOM.
attributes	An array of attributes of an HTML element.
style	An object encapsulating the CSS/HTML styling of an element.

DOM Methods:

DOM Method	Description
getElementById(id)	Gests the element with a given ID below this point in the DOM.
getElementByTagName(tag)	Gests the elements with a given tag below this point in the DOM.
appendChild(node)	Add the given node to the DOM below this point.
removeChild(node)	Remove the specified child node from the DOM.

5.7 DOM OBJECTS(WINDOW, NAVIGATOR, HISTORY, LOCATION)

1. Window Object:

- The window object represents an open window in a browser. If a document contains frames (<frame>or<iframe>tags), the browser creates one window object for the HTML document and one additional window object for each frame.

Example for window object:

```
<html>
<head>
     <script type="text/javascript">
     function openwindow()
     {
          window.open("welcome.html");
     }
     </script>
</head>
<body>
     <form>
          <input type="button" value="Open" onClick=window.alert()>
          <input type="button" onClick="openwindow()" value="Open Window">
     </form>
</body>
</html>
```

2. Navigator Object:

- The JavaScript navigator object is the object representation of the client Internet browser or web navigator program that is being used. Navigator object is the top level object to all others. The navigator object contains information about the browser.

Example for Navigator object:

```
<!DOCTYPE html>
<head>
<meta charset="ISO-8859-1">
<title>JavaScript Navigator</title>
</head>
<body>
   <script type="text/javascript">
      document.write(navigator.appName + "<br>");
      document.write(navigator.appCodeName + "<br>");
      document.write(navigator.appVersion + "<br>");
      document.write(navigator.cookieEnabled + "<br>");
      document.write(navigator.platform + "<br>");
      document.write(navigator.userAgent + "<br>");
   </script>
</body>
</html>
```

3. History Object:

- The history object is automatically created by the JavaScript runtime engine and consists of an array of URLs. These URLs are the URLs the user has visited within a browser window. The history object is part of the Window object and is accessed through the window.history property.

Example for History object:

```
<!DOCTYPE HTML>
<html>
<head>
<title>JavaScript History Object</title>
<script type="text/javascript">
function dispCount()
{
var historyCount = history.length;
alert("Hi, you have visited " + historyCount + " web pages so far.");
}
</script>
</head>
```

```
<body>
<h3>JavaScript History Object Example</h3>
<form>
<input type="button" name="history" value="My History"
onclick="dispCount()">
</form>
</body>
</html>
```

4. Location Object:

- The location object is actually a JavaScript object, not an HTML DOM object. The location object is automatically created by the JavaScript run-time engine and contains information about the current URL. The location object is part of the Window object and is accessed through the window.location property.

Example for Location object:

```
<!DOCTYPE HTML>
<html>
<head>
    <script type="text/javascript">
      function AnalyzeLocation ()
      {
           var message = "";
           message += "hash: " + location.hash + "\n";
           message += "host: " + location.host + "\n";
           message += "hostname: " + location.hostname + "\n";
           message += "href: " + location.href + "\n";
           message += "pathname: " + location.pathname + "\n";
           message += "port: " + location.port + "\n";
           message += "protocol: " + location.protocol + "\n";
           message += "search: " + location.search + "\n";
           alert (message);
      }
    </script>
</head>
<body>
    <button onclick="AnalyzeLocation ();">Analyze the location of the
current document</button>
</body>
</html>
```

5.8 PREDEFINED FUNCTIONS

- Functions are one of the fundamental building blocks in JavaScript. In JavaScript Predefined functions also called as Built-in Functions.
- JavaScript also has four built-in objects like Array, Date, Math, and String. Each object has special-purpose properties and methods associated with it.

5.8.1 String Functions [S-17, W-17]

- The string object is used for storing and manipulating text.
- A string simply stores a series of characters like "Nirali Prakashan".
- A string can be any text inside quotes and we can use simple or double quotes as:

```
var carname="Alto XC60";
var carname='Alto XC60';
```

- The String object let's us work with a series of characters and wraps Javascript's string primitive data type with a number of helper methods.
- Because Javascript automatically converts between string primitives and string objects, we can call any of the helper methods of the string object on a string primitive.

  Syntax: Creating a string object use following syntax:

```
var val = new String(string);
```

- The string parameter is series of characters that has been properly encoded.

String Properties:

Property	Description
1. `constructor`	This property returns a reference to the String function that created the object.
2. `length`	This property returns the length of the string.
3. `prototype`	This property allows we to add properties and methods to an object.

String Methods:

Method Name	Description
1. `charAt()`	This method returns the character at the specified index.
2. `charCodeAt()`	This method returns a number indicating the Unicode value of the character at the given index.
3. `concat()`	This method combines the text of two strings and returns a new string.
4. `indexOf()`	This method returns the index within the calling string object of the first occurrence of the specified value, or –1 if not found.

contd. ...

5. `lastIndexOf()`	This method returns the index within the calling string object of the last occurrence of the specified value, or −1 if not found.
6. `localeCompare()`	This method returns a number indicating whether a reference string comes before or after or is the same as the given string in sort order.
7. `match()`	This method used to match a regular expression against a string.
8. `replace()`	This method used to find a match between a regular expression and a string, and to replace the matched substring with a new substring.
9. `search()`	This method executes the search for a match between a regular expression and a specified string.
10. `slice()`	This method extracts a section of a string and returns a new string.
11. `split()`	This method splits a string object into an array of strings by separating the string into substrings.
12. `substr()`	This method returns the characters in a string beginning at the specified location through the specified number of characters.
13. `substring()`	This method returns the characters in a string between two indexes into the string.
14. `toLocaleLowerCase()`	This method returns the characters within a string are converted to lower case while respecting the current locale.
15. `toLocaleUpperCase()`	This method returns the characters within a string are converted to upper case while respecting the current locale.
16. `toLowerCase()`	This method returns the calling string value converted to lower case.
17. `toString()`	This method returns a string representing the specified object.
18. `toUpperCase()`	This method returns the calling string value converted to uppercase.
19. `valueOf()`	This method returns the primitive value of the specified object.

1. **The length of a string (a String object) is found in the built in property length().**

```
<!DOCTYPE html>
<body>
<script>
var txt = "Hello JavaScript World!";
document.write("<p>" + txt.length + "</p>");
var txt="Amar and Akbar";
document.write("<p>" + txt.length + "</p>");
</script>
</body>
</html>
```

2. **A string is converted to upper/lower case with the methods toUpperCase() / toLowerCase():**

```
<!DOCTYPE html>
<body>
<script>
var txt="Hello JavaScript World!";
document.write("<p>" + txt.toUpperCase() + "</p>");
document.write("<p>" + txt.toLowerCase() + "</p>");
document.write("<p>" + txt + "</p>");
</script>
<p>
The methods returns a new string.
The original string is not changed.
</p>
</body>
</html>
```

3. **Example of concating string.**

```
<html>
<head>
<title>JavaScript String concat() Method</title>
</head>
<body>
<script type="text/javascript">
var str1 = new String( "Prajakta" );
var str2 = new String( "khatavkar" );
var str3 = str1.concat( str2 );
document.write("Concatenated String:" + str3);
</script>
</body>
</html>
```

Output:

```
Concatenated String:Prajaktakhatavkar
```

5.8.2 Math Functions [W-16]

- The math object provides properties and methods for mathematical constants and functions.
- Unlike the other global objects, Math is not a constructor. All properties and methods of Math are static and can be called by using Math as an object without creating it.
- Thus, we refer to the constant pi as Math.PI and we call the sine function as Math.sin(x), where x is the method's argument.

Syntax:

```
var pi_val = Math.PI;
var sine_val = Math.sin(30);
```

Math Properties:

Property	Description
1. E	Euler's constant and the base of natural logarithms, (approximately 2.718).
2. LN2	Natural logarithm of 2, (approximately 0.693).
3. LN10	Natural logarithm of 10, (approximately 2.302).
4. LOG2E	Base 2 logarithm of E, (approximately 1.442).
5. LOG10E	Base 10 logarithm of E, (approximately 0.434).
6. PI	Ratio of the circumference of a circle to its diameter, (approximately 3.14159).
7. SQRT1_2	Square root of 1/2; equivalently, 1 over the square root of 2, (approximately 0.707).
8. SQRT2	Square root of 2, (approximately 1.414).

Math Methods:

Methods	Description
1. abs()	This method returns the absolute value of a number.
2. acos()	This method returns the arccosine (in radians) of a number.
3. asin()	This method returns the arcsine (in radians) of a number.
4. atan()	This method returns the arctangent (in radians) of a number.
5. atan2()	This method returns the arctangent of the quotient of its arguments.
6. ceil()	This method returns the smallest integer greater than or equal to a number.
7. cos()	This method returns the cosine of a number.
8. exp()	This method returns E^N, where N is the argument, and E is Euler's constant, the base of the natural logarithm.

contd. ...

9. `floor()`	This method returns the largest integer less than or equal to a number.
10. `log()`	This method returns the natural logarithm (base E) of a number.
11. `max()`	This method returns the largest of zero or more numbers.
12. `min()`	This method returns the smallest of zero or more numbers.
13. `pow()`	This method returns base to the exponent power, that is, base exponent.
14. `random()`	This method returns a pseudo-random number between 0 and 1.
15. `round()`	This method returns the value of a number rounded to the nearest integer.
16. `sin()`	This method returns the sine of a number.
17. `sqrt()`	This method returns the square root of a number.
18. `tan()`	This method returns the tangent of a number.
19. `toSource()`	This method returns the string "Math".

Example: Write a program to returns the square root of the given number.

```
<!DOCTYPE html>
<html>
<body>
Square Root of 64 is: <span id="p1"></span>
<script>
document.getElementById('p1').innerHTML=Math.sqrt(17);
</script>
</body>
</html>
```

Output:

```
Square Root of 64 is: 4.12
```

5.9 ARRAY IN JAVASCRIPT [S-18]

- Array is used to store a set of values in a single variable name.
- Arrays are a fundamental part of most programming languages and scripting languages. Arrays are simply an ordered stack of data items with the same data type.
- Using arrays, we can store multiple values under a single name. Instead of using a separate variable for each item, we can use one array to hold all of them.
- An array is a special variable, which can hold more than one value at a time.

Creating Arrays in JavaScript (Single-dimensional):

- Most programming languages use similar syntax to create arrays. JavaScript arrays are created by first assigning an array object to a variable name.
- Array are objects which can store multiple values of same type, unlike variables which only store a single value at a time.
- Since, array is an object, its syntax is same as synatx used in creating a new object.

  Syntax: `var variableName = new Array(val1, val2, ....... valn );`

- Accessing an array value is quite easy. We use array index to access a value.
- If we want to access val1 from the above syntax, we use Array[0]. So,

```
Array[0] holds val1
Array[1] holds val2
Array[3] holds val3
......
Array[n] holds valn
```

Creating Two Dimensional Arrays:

- Generally, creating two dimensional arrays is very similar to creating one dimensional arrays. Some languages allow us to create two dimensional arrays simply by adding an index item, however JavaScript does not support two dimensional arrays.
- JavaScript, does however, allow us to simulate a two dimensional array. We can do this by creating an "array of an array".
- To do this, we create an array, loop through the array, and for each element, we create another array. Then, we simply add an index for each column of our grid. In JavaSript this would look something like this:

```
var faq = new Array(2)
for (i=0; i &lt;2; i++)
faq[i]=new Array(2)
faq[0][1] = "Arrays"
faq[0][2] = "What is an array?"
faq[1][1] = "Arrays"
faq[1][2] = "How to create arrays?"
faq[2][1] = "Arrays"
faq[2][2] = "What are two dimensional arrays?"
```

Array Methods:

Method	Description
1. concat()	This method returns a new array comprised of this array joined with other arrays and/or values.
2. every()	This method returns true if every element in this array satisfies the provided testing function.
3. filter()	This method creates a new array with all of the elements of this array for which the provided filtering function returns true.
4. forEach()	This method calls a function for each element in the array.
5. indexOf()	This method returns the first (least) index of an element within the array equal to the specified value, or -1 if none is found.
6. join()	This method joins all elements of an array into a string.

contd. ...

7. `lastIndexOf()`	This method returns the last (greatest) index of an element within the array equal to the specified value, or -1 if none is found.
8. `map()`	This method creates a new array with the results of calling a provided function on every element in this array.
9. `pop()`	This method removes the last element from an array and returns that element.
10. `push()`	This method adds one or more elements to the end of an array and returns the new length of the array.
11. `reduce()`	This method apply a function simultaneously against two values of the array (from left-to-right) as to reduce it to a single value.
12. `reduceRight()`	This method apply a function simultaneously against two values of the array (from right-to-left) as to reduce it to a single value.
13. `reverse()`	This method reverses the order of the elements of an array -- the first becomes the last, and the last becomes the first.
14. `shift()`	This method removes the first element from an array and returns that element.
15. `slice()`	This method extracts a section of an array and returns a new array.
16. `some()`	This method returns true if at least one element in this array satisfies the provided testing function.
17. `toSource()`	This method represents the source code of an object.
18. `sort()`	This method sorts the elements of an array.
19. `splice()`	This method adds and/or removes elements from an array.
20. `toString()`	This method returns a string representing the array and its elements.
21. `unshift()`	This method adds one or more elements to the front of an array and returns the new length of the array.

1. Example for concat() array method:

```
<!DOCTYPE html>
<head>
<title>JavaScript Array concat() Method</title>
</head>
<body>
<script type="text/javascript">
   var alpha = ["x", "y", "z"];
```

```
    var numeric = [1, 2, 3];
    var alphaNumeric = alpha.concat(numeric);
    document.write("alphaNumeric: " + alphaNumeric );
</script>
</body>
</html>
```

2. Example of sort() method:

```
<!DOCTYPE html>
<head>
<title>JavaScript Array sort() Method</title>
</head>
<body>
<script type="text/javascript">
var arr = new Array("orange", "mango", "banana", "apple");
var sorted = arr.sort();
document.write("Returned string is: " + sorted );
</script>
</body>
</html>
```

5.10 EVENT HANDLING IN JAVASCRIPT [S-18, 19]

Events:

- JavaScript-enabled web pages are typically event driven. Events are actions that occur on the web page. Generally speaking they occur when.
- Events are signals generated when specific action occur.
- JavaScript is aware of these signals are scripts can be built to react to these events.

Event Handler:

- Event handlers execute JavaScript code to respond to events whenever they occur.
- Event handlers are scripts, in the form of attributes of specific HTML tags, which we as the programmer can write.
- The general form of an event handler is:

```
<html_tag other_attributes eventhandler = "JavaScript program">
```

- Event handler is actually a call to a function defined in the header of the document or a single JavaScript command. While any JavaScript statements, methods or functions can appear inside the quotation marks of event handler.

Creating an Event Handler:

- We do not need the <script> tag to define an event handler. Instead, we add an event attribute to an individual HTML tag.

- For example, here is a link that includes an OnMouseOver event handler.

```
<a href=http://www.pragati.com/" OnMouseOver="Window.alert ("We moved over the link");Click here </a>
```

- Here, <a> is tag, which specifies a statement to be used as OnMouseOver event handler for the link and this statement displays an alert message when the mouse moves over the link.
- We can use JavaScript statements like the previous one in an event handler, but if we need more than one statement, its good idea to use a function as the event handler like this:

```
<a href = "#bottom" OnMouseOver = "DoIt();">
```

- Move the mouse over this link </a>
- This example calls a function called DoIt() when the user moves the mouse over the link.

Event Handlers with JavaScript:

- Instead of specifying an event handler is an HTML document, we can use JavaScript to assign a function as an event handler. This allows us to set event handlers.
- To define event handler in this way, first define a function and then assign it is an event handler.

Example for event handlers with JavaScript.

```
<!DOCTYPE html>
<head><title> Events</title>
<script>
function react()
{
alert("Please enter any value");
}
</script></head>
<body>
document.onMousedown=react;
</body>
</html>
```

- Events are occurrences generated by the browser, such as loading a document or by the user such as moving the mouse.
- They are the user and browser activities to which we may respond dynamically with a scripting language like JavaScript.

1. onclick Event:

- onclick is the most frequently used event type which occurs when a user clicks mouse left button.
- We can put our validation, warning and so on against this event type.

Example for onclick event in JavaScript.

```
<!DOCTYPE html>
<head>
<script type="text/javascript">
function sayHello()
{
   alert("Hello JavaScript World!")
}
</script>
</head>
<body>
<script type="text/javascript">
<!--
document.write("Hello JavaScript World!")
//-->
</script>
<input type="button" onclick="sayHello()" value="Say Hello" />
</body>
</html>
```

2. onsubmit Event:

- onsubmit is another most important event type.
- This event occurs when we try to submit a form. So we can put our form validation against this event type.
- Following is a simple example showing its usage. Here, we are calling a validate() function before submitting a form data to the web server. If validate() function returns true the form will be submitted otherwise it will not submit the data.

Example for onsubmit event in JavaScript.

```
<!DOCTYPE html>
<html>
<body>
<p>click on submit button</p>
<form action="/action_page.php" onsubmit="myFunction()">
  Enter name: <input type="text" name="fname">
  <input type="submit" value="Submit">
</form>
<script>
function myFunction()
{
  alert("The form was submitted");
}
</script>
</body>
</html>
```

3. onmouseover and onmouseout:

- These two event types will help us to create nice effects with images or even with text as well.
- The onMouseover event occurs when we bring our mouse over any element and the onMouseout occurs when we take our mouse out from that element.

Example for onmouseover and mouseout event in JavaScript.

```
<!DOCTYPE html>
<html>
<body>
<img onmouseover="bigImg(this)" onmouseout="normalImg(this)" border="0"
src="smiley.gif" alt="Smiley" width="32" height="32">
<p>The function bigImg() is triggered when the user moves the mouse pointer
over the image.</p>
<p>The function normalImg() is triggered when the mouse pointer is moved
out of the image.</p>
<script>
function bigImg(x)
{
  x.style.height = "64px";
  x.style.width = "64px";
}
function normalImg(x)
{
  x.style.height = "32px";
  x.style.width = "32px";
}
</script>
</body>
</html>
```

4. onload and onunload Events:

- These two events are triggered when the user enters or leaves the page.
- The onload event can be used to check the visitor's browser type and browser version, and load the proper version of the web page based on the information.
- The onload and onunload events can be used to deal with cookies.

Example for onload and onunload event in JavaScript.

```
<!DOCTYPE html>
<html>
<body onload="myFunction()">
<h1>Hello World!</h1>
```

```
<script>
function myFunction()
{
  alert("Page is loaded");
}
</script>
</body>
</html>
Example: Example for onunload event.
<!DOCTYPE html>
<html>
<body onunload="myFunction()">
<h1>Welcome to my Home Page</h1>
<script>
function myFunction()
{
  alert("Thank you for visiting W3Schools!");
}
</script>
</body>
</html>
```

5. onchange Event:

- This event are often used in combination with validation of input fields.
- Following is an example of how to use the onchange. The upperCase() function will be called when a user changes the content of an input field.

Example for onchange event in JavaScript.

```
<!DOCTYPE html>
<html>
<head>
<script>
function myFunction()
{
  var x = document.getElementById("mySelect").value;
  document.getElementById("demo").innerHTML = "You selected: " + x;
}
</script>
</head>
<body>
<p>Select a new car from the list.</p>
```

```
<select id="mySelect" onchange="myFunction()">
  <option value="Audi">Audi</option>
  <option value="BMW">BMW</option>
  <option value="Mercedes">Mercedes</option>
  <option value="Volvo">Volvo</option>
</select>
<p>When you select a new car, a function is triggered which outputs the value of the selected car.</p>
<p id="demo"></p>
</body>
</html>
```

6. onmousedown and onmouseup Events:

- These three events are all parts of a mouse-click.
- First when a mouse-button is clicked, the onmousedown event is triggered, then, when the mouse-button is released, the onmouseup event is triggered, finally, when the mouse-click is completed, the onclick event is triggered.

Example for onmousedown, onmouseup event in JavaScript.

```
<!DOCTYPE html>
<html>
<head>
<script>
function mouseDown() {
  document.getElementById("myP").style.color = "red";
}
function mouseUp() {
  document.getElementById("myP").style.color = "green";
}
</script>
</head>
<body>
<p id="myP" onmousedown="mouseDown()" onmouseup="mouseUp()">
Click the text! The mouseDown() function is triggered when the mouse button is pressed down over this paragraph, and sets the color of the text to red. The mouseUp() function is triggered when the mouse button is released, and sets the color of the text to green.
</p>
</body>
</html>
```

5.11 PROGRAMS

1. Write a javascript program to read a number from user store its factors into the array and display the array.(onclick Event). **[S-18, 19]**

Ans.
```
<html>
  <body>
   <script type="text/javascript">
     function factors()
     {
      var arr = [];
      var str = document.getElementById("str").value;
      for(var i=0;i<=str;i++)
      {
          if(str%i==0)
         {
            arr.push(i);
         }
      }
      document.getElementById('result').innerHTML = arr;
   }
   </script>
   <form>
        Enter a Number: <input type="text" id="str" name="string" /><br />
        <input type="submit" value="Check" onclick="factors();"/>
         <div style="margin-top: 10px;" id="result"></div>
   </form>
</body>
</html>
```

2. Write a javascript program to design student registration form and perform the following validation.

(i) Check all field should not contain NULL value.

(ii) Check name field contain only alphabets.

(iii) Mobile no. field should be of 10 digits. **[S-19]**

Ans.
```
<html>
  <head>
     <title>Form Validation</title>
     <script type = "text/javascript">
     function validate()
     {
        //validation for Name not null and for alphabet
        if( document.myForm.Name.value == "" )
        {
```

```
        alert( "Please provide your name!" );
        document.myForm.Name.focus() ;
        return false;
    }
    else
    {
        var regex = /^[a-zA-Z\s]+$/;
        if(regex.test(document.myForm.Name.value) == false)
        {
        alert("Please enter a valid name");
        }
    }
    // validation for email not null and email format
    if( document.myForm.EMail.value == "" )
    {
        alert( "Please provide your Email!" );
        document.myForm.EMail.focus() ;
        return false;
    }
    else
    {
        var regex = /^\S+@\S+\.\S+$/;
        if(regex.test(document.myForm.EMail.value) === false)
        {
        alert("Please enter a valid email address");
        }
    }
    // validation for mobile number
    if( document.myForm.Mobile.value == "" ||
                                isNaN( document.myForm.Mobile.value ) ||
        document.myForm.Mobile.value.length != 10 )
    {
        alert( "Please provide a Mobile number in
                                              the format ##########." );
        document.myForm.Mobile.focus() ;
        return false;
    }
    // validation for Zip code
    if( document.myForm.Zip.value == "" ||
                                   isNaN( document.myForm.Zip.value ) ||
        document.myForm.Zip.value.length != 5 )
```

```
        {
            alert( "Please provide a zip in the format #####." );
            document.myForm.Zip.focus() ;
            return false;
        }
    }
    </script>
</head>
<body>
    <form name = "myForm" onsubmit = "return(validate());">
        <table cellspacing = "2" cellpadding = "2" border = "1">

            <tr>
                <td align = "right">Name</td>
                <td><input type = "text" name = "Name" /></td>
            </tr>

            <tr>
                <td align = "right">EMail</td>
                <td><input type = "text" name = "EMail" /></td>
            </tr>

            <tr>
                <td align = "right">Mobile Number</td>
                <td><input type = "text" name = "Mobile" /></td>
            </tr>

            <tr>
                <td align = "right">Zip Code</td>
                <td><input type = "text" name = "Zip" /></td>
            </tr>

            <tr>
                <td align = "right"></td>
                <td><input type = "submit" value = "Submit" /></td>
            </tr>
        </table>
    </form>
</body>
</html>
```

3. Write a javascript program to create four color button on the web page. Clicking on button will change the background color of web page. **[S-17, 19]**

Ans.

```
<!DOCTYPE html>
<html lang="en">
<head>
<meta charset="utf-8">
<title>Change the Background Color with JavaScript</title>
<script>
    function changeBodyBg(color)
    {
        document.body.style.background = color;
    }
</script>
</head>
<body>
    <div>
        <label>Change Webpage Background To:</label>
        <button type="button"
        onclick="changeBodyBg('yellow');">Yellow</button>
        <button type="button"
        onclick="changeBodyBg('lime');">Lime</button>
        <button type="button"
        onclick="changeBodyBg('orange');">Orange</button>
        <button type="button"
        onclick="changeBodyBg('red');">Red</button>
    </div>
    <br>
</body>
</html>
```

4. Write a Javascript to create an image slider (use array to store images). **[S-18]**

Ans. Refer to Section

```
<script language="JavaScript">
var i = 0;
var path = new Array();
// LIST OF IMAGES
path[0] = "image_1.gif";
path[1] = "image_2.gif";
path[2] = "image_3.gif";
```

```
function swapImage()
{
   document.slide.src = path[i];
   if(i < path.length - 1) i++; else i = 0;
   setTimeout("swapImage()",3000);
}
window.onload=swapImage;
</script>
<img height="200" name="slide" src="image_1.gif" width="400" />
```

5. Write javascript program to check number is palindrome or not.

Ans.

```
<html>
   <body>
      <script type="text/javascript">
        function Palindrome()
        {
         var revStr = "";
         var str = document.getElementById("str").value;
         var i = str.length;
         for(var j=i; j>=0; j--)
         {
            revStr = revStr+str.charAt(j);
          }
         if(str == revStr)
         {
            alert(str+" -is Palindrome");
          }
         else
         {
            alert(str+" -is not a Palindrome");
         }
      }
      </script>
      <form >
            Enter a String/Number: <input type="text" id="str"
   name="string" /><br />
            <input type="submit" value="Check" onclick="Palindrome();"/>
      </form>
   </body>
</html>
```

6. Write javascript program to check given number is perfect or not. **[W-16, 17]**

Ans.

```
<html>
<head><TITLE></TITLE>
<script language="JavaScript">
    var a=prompt("enter a value");
    var z=a;
    var c=0;
    for(var i=1;i<a;i++)
    {
        if(a%i==0)
        {
            c=c+i;
        }
    }
    if(c==z)
    {
        alert("given no is perfect");
    }
    else
    {
        alert("given no is not a perfect");
    }
</script>
</head>
<body></body>
</html>
```

7. Write a JavaScript program to find x^n.

Ans.

```
<html>
<body>
<script>
function power(x, y)
{
   var i=1;
   var p=1;
   for(i=1;i<=y;i++)
   {
      p=p*x;
   }
   alert("power is:"+p);
}
</script>
</body>
<input type="Button" onclick="power(4,3)" value="Power is">
</html>
```

8. Write a program to find factorial of number.

Ans.

```
<html>
 <body>
  <script>
  function fact(n)
  {
     var f=1;
     for(i=1;i<=n;i++)
     {
        f=f*i;
     }
     document.write(+f);
  }
  var ff = fact(5);
  </script>
</body>
</html>
```

Summary

- JavaScript is a platform independent object-based scripting language.
- Client-side JavaScript is the name given to JavaScript code that is executed by a web browser on client machine.
- JavaScript is a case-sensitive language and all the statements are written in lower case.
- JavaScript allows omitting semicolon when statements are placed in separate lines. If we combine statements into a single line, we must use semicolon to separate them.
- document.write is a standard JavaScript command for producing output to a document window.
- A variable is a container of values or string. The values stored in a variable can be accessed using the variable name.
- JavaScript supports three primitive data types: number, string and boolean. JavaScript allows two composite data types: objects and arrays.
- An if statement is used to execute a statement or a block of statements on the basis of condition.
- A switch statement in JavaScript is used to perform different actions based on different conditions. It can be a replacement for multiple if... else if... statement.
- Loop statements tell JavaScript interpreter to execute same statements again and again until a specified condition is met.
- The for loop consists of three optional expressions. It executes block statement repeatedly again and again until the condition is false.
- The while loop statement is simpler than for loop. It repeats block statement again and again until the specified condition is false.
- Unlike while loop, do-while loop always executes a block of code at least once.
- Instead of exiting a loop, continue statement skips the statement following it and restarts a loop in a new iteration.

Check Your Understanding

1. JavaScript is ______ language.
   (a) Scripting (b) None of These
   (c) Programming (d) Application
2. ______ JavaScript is also called client-side JavaScript.
   (a) Microsoft (b) Navigator
   (c) LiveWire (d) Native
3. What should appear at the very end of your JavaScript?
   The <script LANGUAGE="JavaScript">tag
   (a) The </script> (b) The <script>
   (c) The END statement (d) None of the above
4. Which of the following can't be done with client-side JavaScript?
   (a) Validating a form.
   (b) Sending a form's contents by email.
   (c) Storing the form's contents to a database file on the server.
   (d) None of the above.
5. To which object does the location property belong?
   (a) Window (b) Position
   (c) Element (d) Location
6. What is the result of the following code snippet?
   ```
   window.location === document.location
   ```
   (a) False (b) True
   (c) 0 (d) 1
7. What does the location property represent?
   (a) Current DOM object (b) Current URL
   (c) Both DOM object and URL (d) None of the mentioned

Answers

1. (a)	2. (b)	3. (a)	4. (c)	5. (a)	6. (b)	7. (a)

Practice Questions

Q.1 Answer the following Question in short.

1. What is JavaScript?
2. What is a function? How to create it?
3. Enlist various operators in JavaScript.
4. Explain number function with syntax.
5. What is event?

Q.2 Answer the following Question in detail.

1. Describe navigation object with example.
2. What is meant by array? How to define an array.
3. What is event? Explain event handling in JavaScript.
4. Create a personal home page named home.html with the following content:

5. Our name written in the <title> and an <h1> tag at the top.
6. A picture of yourself after or next to the heading. If we do not have a digital picture of yourself, use clip art or a favourite landscape.
7. Create a home page named toy Store.html for a company that sells toys. Include images of balls, jacks, whistles, skateboards, dolls, and other items that the toy company sells. We should be able to find the images we need from an online clip art library.
8. Write a program to display even and odd number between 1 to 20.
9. Explain various control statement statement with example.
10. What is a loop? What are its types? Explain with example.
11. Write short notes on: (i) math object, (ii) string object.
12. What is function? How to create and call it? Explain with example.
13. Write a program for finding prime numbers using functions.
14. Explain DOM object in detail.

Q.3 Define the following terms.

1. Array
2. Function
3. Event
4. Client side scripting
5. Server side scripting.

Previous Exams Questions

Summer 2019

1. Name any two events associated with mouse. **[2 M]**

Ans. Refer to Section 5.10.

2. Write a javascript program to read a number from user store its factors into the array and display the array.(onclick Event) **[4 M]**

Ans. Refer to Section 5.11, Program 1.

3. Write a javascript program to design student registration form and perform the following validation. **[4 M]**

(i) Check all field should not contain NULL value.

(ii) Check name field contain only alphabets.

(iii) Mobile no. field should be of 10 digits.

Ans. Refer to Section 5.11, Program 2.

4. Write a javascript program to create four color button on the web page. Clicking on button will change the background color of web page. **[4 M]**

Ans. Refer to Section 5.11, Program 3.

Summer 2018

1. Explain javascript array methods. **[2 M]**

Ans. Refer to Section 5.9.

2. Name of any two events associated with mouse. **[2 M]**

Ans. Refer to Section 5.10.

3. Explain event handling in Javascript. **[4 M]**

Ans. Refer to Section 5.10.

4. Explain DOM in Javascript. **[4 M]**

Ans. Refer to Section 5.6.

5. Write a Javascript to create an image slider (use array to store images). **[4 M]**

Ans. Refer to Section 5.11, Program 4.

6. Write a Javascript program to read a number from user, store its factors into the array and display that array. **[4 M]**

Ans. Refer to Section 5.11, Program 1.

Winter 2017

1. List any two string functions in Javascript. **[2 M]**

Ans. Refer to Section 5.8.1.

2. Write a JavaScript program to check given number is perfect or not. **[4 M]**

Ans. Refer to Section 5.11, Program 6.

3. Write a note on DOM. **[4 M]**

Ans. Refer to Section 5.6.

4. Write a JavaScript program to check whether a given number is prime or note. **[4 M]**

Ans. Refer to Section 5.11, Program 6.

Summer 2017

1. Explain any two string functions in JavaScript. **[2 M]**

Ans. Refer to Section 5.8.1.

2. Write a note on DOM. **[4 M]**

Ans. Refer to Section 5.6.

3. Write a JavaScript program to create four button on the webpage. Clicking on button will change the background colour of web page. **[4 M]**

Ans. Refer to Section 5.11, Program 3.

Winter 2016

1. List any four Math functions in JavaScript. **[2 M]**

Ans. Refer to Section 5.8.2.

2. Write a JavaScript program to check given number is perfect or not. **[4 M]**

Ans. Refer to Section 5.11, Program 6.

3. Write a note on DOM. **[4 M]**

Ans. Refer to Section 5.6.

4. Write a JavaScript program to check whether a given number is prime or not. **[4 M]**

Ans. Refer to Section 5.11, Program 6.

■■■